CYBER INSECURITY

CYBER INSECURITY

The Silent Risk in Your Boardroom

DR. KIRAN KEWALRAMANI

NU VOICE
PRESS

NU VOICE PRESS

First published by NU VOICE PRESS 2025
An imprint of Hubhawks Pvt. Ltd
www.nuvoicepress.com

This is a work of fiction. Space and time have been rearranged to suit the convenience of the book. Except for public figures, hotels, and institution names, any resemblance to persons living or dead or the real events are purely coincidental. The opinions expressed in the book are those of the characters, and should not be confused with that of the Author.

ISBN: 978-81-988726-5-4

Typeset by Saanvi Graphics, Noida
Printed at Thomson Press
Published by Nu Voice Press

Disclaimer

This publication is for general information only and is not intended as legal, financial or professional advice. Readers should seek independent advice specific to their circumstances. The author accepts no liability for any loss or damage arising from reliance on the content. References to real-world events and organisations are based on publicly available information and used solely for illustrative purposes. All views expressed are those of the author.

Dedication

This book is dedicated to the people who have been my anchor, my motivation and my constant source of strength. To my beloved wife and son, your patience, encouragement and belief in me made this journey possible. To my dad, whose values shaped my foundation, and to my mother, whose quiet resilience continues to guide me. To my godmother, whose unwavering faith in me has never wavered, and to my sister and brother-in-law, my father-in-law and mother-in-law, whose support I carry with deep gratitude.

I also want to acknowledge the many individuals I've learned from throughout my cybersecurity journey, not just for the insights they shared, but also for the lessons in what leadership should and should not be.

This book reflects a mission that sits at the core of who I am: to strengthen the cybersecurity posture of every organisation, regardless of size or sector. It is why I stepped away from the CIO seat and founded *Cyber Ethos*. Because I believe that true cyber resilience begins in the boardroom. When Directors and Executives lead with clarity and conviction, we begin to shift the cyber culture, and that's when we start to win.

Praise for the Author

"Kiran Kewalramani and Cyber Ethos have helped enhance Metro's cyber posture, providing us with both practical solutions and expert advice. We look forward to continuing to work with Cyber Ethos to further build and strengthen our cybersecurity framework in this complex and rapidly changing environment."

–**Robin Bates**, General Counsel and Company Secretary, Metro Mining

"I worked with Kiran whilst he was engaged at the NSWPF. Kiran is an extremely knowledgeable manager with expertise in Project Quality Assurance, Project Governance and Project/ Program methodologies. The key attributes I found Kiran to have were 'initiative' and an innate capability to determine alignments at both strategic and tactical levels. This greatly assisted the Operational Policing Program in determining future dependencies, allowing a much earlier stakeholder engagement process both internally and with external agencies. Team player with multiple Programs and Projects."

–**Keith Willott**, Retired Chief Inspector, NSW Police. Currently Chairman of the Kundabung Public Land Reserve Land Manager Board

"Kiran Kewalramani facilitated and delivered a cybersecurity awareness training for our team. His ability to communicate cybersecurity concepts in plain English increased our team's awareness. Kiran delivered practical insights that enhanced our cyber hygiene practices, strengthening our firm's cybersecurity resilience."

–**Tina Zawila**, Director, UHY Haines Norton Gladstone

"Kiran Kewalramani has provided a comprehensive ISO27K and Essential 8-based Right Fit for Risk (RFFR) baseline assessment for Roseberry, Queensland. The RFFR program has been a requirement from the Department of Education, Skills and Employment (DESE) – an Australian Federal Govt department. Based on the findings and guidance from Kiran, we have improved our Essential 8 maturity to protect our environment. Under Kiran's leadership, Cyber Ethos is bound to thrive and excel in the cybersecurity arena. We highly recommend their services."

–**Michelle Coats**, General Manager, Roseberry, Queensland

"Kiran is an amazing business and technology leader who generates wonderful followership with his team. I have known and worked with Kiran for one and a half years at the NSW Rural Fire Service and have always admired his leadership style and business acumen. He is that rare leader who skilfully balances driving outstanding business results through technology. He continually motivates employees who will go the extra mile for him. Kiran is a consummate professional with high standards and integrity, and I know he will make an immediate impact in his next company and/or future professional endeavours."

– **Amit Taneja**, Principal Technical Lead/Manager/Delivery Lead/Solutions Architect/Scrum Master/Product Owner

"Kiran is a great professional, having a passion for excellence in everything he delivers. Kiran is candid in his communications and reaches the teams across the globe and functions boundaryless. He was able to always find a way to accomplish things by cutting through the hurdles and focusing on the outcome. He understands how to turn business needs into real-world solutions. He has a strong technical background and uses his exceptional business skills to develop a range of solutions that suit business needs. I would hire him back any day."

–**Frances Strutt**, CEO – Chief Exploration Officer

Preface

"Cybersecurity isn't just an IT issue. It's a Boardroom blind spot and a leadership responsibility. The faster we realise this, the fewer headlines we'll have to explain."

– Dr Kiran Kewalramani

CYBERSECURITY HAS ALWAYS BEEN CLOSE to my heart, not just as a profession, but as a purpose. After spending over two decades in technology leadership roles, including time as a Chief Information Officer (CIO) and Chief Information Security Officer (CISO), I've seen firsthand how cyber risk has evolved from a technical concern to a boardroom imperative.

Too often, I've watched Directors and Audit & Risk Committee (ARC) members wrestle with the weight of responsibility yet feel unequipped to govern cybersecurity with confidence. It's not due to a lack of intelligence or intent; it's a lack of translation. The language of cyber is rarely spoken in the boardroom, and this disconnect puts organisations at risk.

I wrote this book to close that gap. It brings together the lessons I've learned on both sides of the table, helping boards understand what matters, what to ask, and how to lead in an era driven by technology and Artificial Intelligence (AI), where resilience starts at the top.

If you are a Director seeking clarity, an audit and risk committee member looking for the right questions, or simply a leader who understands that trust is built on good governance, I hope this guide serves you well.

Because when boards step up, organisations don't just survive, they thrive.

Table of Contents

Introduction

WHEN WAS THE LAST TIME you really thought about cybersecurity, beyond ticking a compliance box or skimming an IT report?

I'm Dr Kiran Kewalramani, and I'm here to challenge you: cybersecurity is no longer a spectator sport for Directors; it's a fundamental business imperative that demands your active involvement.

Over 25 years in cybersecurity leadership has shown me that the biggest cyber breaches aren't caused by technological failures – they happen due to boardroom blind spots. Often, Directors underestimate the urgency and scale of cyber threats, relegating cybersecurity to mere IT concerns. But cybersecurity is no longer just an IT issue. It's a core business risk, tightly woven into every aspect of corporate strategy, finance and governance.

In my experience advising boards across multiple sectors, from large ASX[1]-listed corporations to agile small businesses, I've

1 Australian Securities Exchange

seen a recurring pattern. Directors often feel overwhelmed by technical jargon and complexity, leaving them unsure of how to engage effectively. The good news? You don't need to become a cybersecurity expert to govern cybersecurity effectively. However, you do need enough clarity to confidently challenge your technical teams, question assumptions and assess risks with precision.

My purpose in writing this book is straightforward: to eliminate those blind spots once and for all, empowering you to take control of your company's cybersecurity posture. This is not a book loaded with tech-speak – it's your practical roadmap, crafted explicitly for Board Directors. It simplifies complex technical language into clear, actionable insights designed specifically from your perspective, ensuring you grasp the essence of cybersecurity without drowning in technicalities.

Each chapter is strategically designed to strengthen your understanding and decision-making ability. You will learn to justify cybersecurity investments clearly, ensuring every dollar spent contributes meaningfully to your business's resilience. You'll also master how to communicate effectively with your CIO or CISO, bridging the infamous gap between technical teams and the boardroom. Furthermore, you will discover how to confidently navigate your responsibilities around data privacy, compliance and legal implications, critical aspects often overlooked until disaster strikes.

Cyber threats aren't hypothetical – they're immediate and escalating. From ransomware attacks paralysing entire businesses overnight to cloud vulnerabilities exposing sensitive customer information, the reality of cybersecurity risk grows more serious daily. Yet, too often, boards only react after a breach occurs. This reactive posture is dangerous and costly. It's time to shift from reactive firefighting to proactive governance.

Embracing cybersecurity isn't just about mitigating threats; it's about enabling growth, innovation, and maintaining stakeholder trust. Businesses that proactively manage cyber risks don't just survive – they thrive. They gain competitive advantages by demonstrating robust cybersecurity maturity, attracting clients, investors and talent, who demand transparency and security assurance.

I firmly believe cybersecurity decisions made today will shape your company's future successes or failures. And, importantly, they will shape your legacy as a Director. Leadership in the digital age demands courage, clarity and decisive action. By the end of this book, you will not only understand cybersecurity but also appreciate why it's integral to your overall governance strategy.

This journey is not merely academic; it's deeply personal. I've witnessed firsthand the devastating impacts cyber incidents have on businesses, their leaders and their customers. But I've also witnessed the transformative power of boards that proactively embrace cybersecurity as a cornerstone of governance.

Your legacy as a Director begins now, in this moment of choice. Choose proactive engagement. Choose informed leadership.

Choose to build a resilient and secure organisation prepared for the challenges of tomorrow.

Together, let's turn cybersecurity from a daunting unknown into one of your greatest strengths as a leader. Your business, your stakeholders and your reputation depend on it.

Let's begin.

CHAPTER 1

Why Ignoring Cybersecurity is Boardroom Suicide

IN MY YEARS SERVING AS both a Board Advisor and the CIO/CISO[2], I've walked into boardrooms where cybersecurity was barely a line item on the agenda. That was before the breach. Before the regulator's knock. Before the front-page headline. Only then did the board realise that the question wasn't whether cybersecurity was their responsibility, but why they ignored it in the first place.

Cybersecurity today is not a technical problem. It is a strategic, operational and reputational risk that sits squarely within the board's remit. In 2025 and beyond, boards that fail to grasp this truth are not just uninformed – they're negligent.

Whether you're a Director of a listed ASX entity, a national not-for-profit or a family business entering its second generation,

2 Chief Information Officer/Chief Information Security Officer

the landscape is the same. Cyber threats are relentless. The actors are professional. And the damage is far beyond the IT department's scope.

This chapter lays the foundation for what I call 'fit-for-purpose cybersecurity governance'. You don't need to become a cyber expert, but you do need to know enough to ask the right questions, challenge assumptions and steer the organisation toward resilience.

And let me be blunt: if you're not willing to take that on, you shouldn't be sitting on the board.

The Uncomfortable Truth: Cyber Risk Is an Executive Blind Spot

Let's start with some facts. According to Cybersecurity Ventures, a well-regarded cybersecurity research firm, cybercrime is projected to cost the global economy more than $10 trillion annually by 2025. That number is not only staggering, but also accelerating. In Australia alone, we're seeing a growing list of companies whose names are now synonymous with data breaches.

Despite this, only 1.4% of the top 500 public company boards have a current or former CISO on them. Less than 2.4% have a dedicated cybersecurity committee. Nearly two-thirds assign this critical oversight to an already overburdened audit committee (DHR Global, 2023).

This governance gap between the scale of the threat and the rigour of oversight is like running a bank without a finance committee. And yet, many Directors still view cybersecurity as something to delegate to IT, without meaningful board-level challenge or oversight.

As someone who's served as a CIO and now advises boards across sectors, I've seen this dynamic play out too often. The uncomfortable truth is this: cybersecurity is a strategic blind spot for many boards, until it's too late.

Our failure isn't due to a lack of concern – it's a failure of imagination. We over-index on technical metrics, such as phishing test results, patching rates and audit scores, while ignoring the bigger picture: how resilient are we as an organisation when (not if) an attack comes?

Section 180 of the Corporations Act 2001 (Cth) is unambiguous: Directors have a duty to exercise care and diligence. This includes having a reasonable grasp of the threats that could bring the business to its knees. Regulatory bodies such as the ASIC[3] and APRA[4] have reinforced this expectation. Cyber oversight is no longer best practice – it's baseline.

From my own experience, boards that treat cybersecurity as a compliance checkbox often find themselves blindsided when reality hits. Because cyber risk is dynamic, asymmetric

3 Australian Securities and Investments Commission

4 Australian Prudential Regulation Authority

and relentless, no risk register, however comprehensive, can substitute for active, informed governance.

If the board doesn't ask the right questions, if it doesn't hear directly from its CISO, if it fails to pressure test the organisation's incident response plan, it becomes part of the problem.

The time for plausible deniability is over. Digital risk is business risk, and ignoring it is no longer an option.

Cybersecurity: The Strategic Risk Hiding in Plain Sight

It's tempting to think of cyber risk in terms of firewalls and passwords. But that's outdated thinking. The real risk is to your:

- **Business continuity**: A ransomware attack can halt operations for days or weeks.
- **Brand trust**: One data breach can destroy customer loyalty built over decades.
- **Financial position**: Regulatory fines, class actions, remediation, and lost revenue can run into the millions.
- **Licence to operate**: For regulated industries, non-compliance can mean more than fines. It can mean shutdown.

Cyber risk is no longer about systems. It's about strategy. I've advised boards across industries, including mining, government, education and non-profits, and the pattern is always the same: cyber discussions happen after an incident, not before. That's like talking about insurance after your house has already burned down.

A business contact once told me, '*We thought cyber was covered until our supply chain partner got hit, and suddenly we were in the headlines.*' It's a painful way to learn that third-party risk is first-party impact. This is why cyber governance must extend beyond the firewall and into the ecosystem of partners, vendors and digital dependencies.

When the board fails to treat cybersecurity as a strategic issue, the entire business becomes vulnerable. It's not just the CIO's headache; it's your organisation's Achilles heel.

And in today's climate, stakeholders – from customers to investors –are increasingly unwilling to forgive such oversight. Directors are now expected to demonstrate cyber literacy, not just cyber interest.

The strategic question every Director must ask is: *Are we prepared to manage and recover from a cyber event, or are we simply hoping one doesn't happen?*

Because hope is not a strategy. But governance is.

Directors Must Lead from the Front

Cybersecurity leadership starts at the top, and that means the board. Delegation without understanding is not governance; it's abdication. As a Director, you cannot lead what you do not understand, and in the realm of cyber risk, ignorance is not just dangerous, it's indefensible.

I've walked into boardrooms where Directors proudly declare, '*That's why we have IT,* ' as though digital risk is someone else's burden. Let me be clear: this mindset is outdated and risky. Cyber resilience is an enterprise-wide responsibility, and Directors set the tone for how seriously it's taken across the organisation.

Leading from the front means more than attending the annual security update. It means:

- **Challenging assumptions:** Ask your executive team what keeps them up at night. Then ask what's being done about it.
- **Ensuring cybersecurity appears regularly on the board agenda:** This isn't a once-a-year conversation.
- **Insisting on plain-English briefings:** If your CISO can't explain the organisation's risk posture in terms that make sense to you, ask them to try again.
- **Creating space for specialist input:** If cybersecurity is not a core board capability, bring in external advisors or consider appointing someone who has that depth.

Consider this simple litmus test: can each Director on your board answer these five questions with confidence?

- What is our current cyber risk exposure, and how is it measured?

- Do we have a dedicated CISO, and do they have board access?
- What is our cyber incident response plan, and has it been tested this year?
- Are we compliant with relevant regulations (e.g. Privacy Act, CPS 234)?
- How much are we investing in cybersecurity, and is it aligned with our risk appetite?

If the answer to any of these is '*I'm not sure*', then your board has work to do.

I've worked with Directors who've transformed their organisations' posture not by becoming cyber experts, but by taking their fiduciary duty seriously. They read. They questioned. They listened. And crucially, they acted.

Leadership isn't about having the answers – it's about knowing which questions to ask and demanding accountability for the responses.

Because at the end of the day, cyber risk is business risk, and business leadership starts with you.

Governance, Not Guesswork: Frameworks That Work

Directors don't need to reinvent the wheel. There are established frameworks, backed by industry, regulators and international best practice, which provide clear guidance on how to assess, govern and uplift cybersecurity.

ISO/ IEC[5] 27001

The global standard for information security management. It offers a systematic approach to managing sensitive company data, so it remains secure. It includes people, processes and IT systems by applying a risk management process.

NIST Cybersecurity Framework

Developed by the U.S. National Institute of Standards and Technology, this framework helps organisations understand, manage and reduce their cybersecurity risks. It's structured around five core functions: identify, protect, detect, respond and recover.

APRA CPS 234

For APRA-regulated entities, these prudential standards mandate that boards ensure their information security capabilities are commensurate with the size and extent of threats. It explicitly holds boards accountable for oversight.

SMB[6] 1001:2025 – The Director's Cyber Governance Standard

---

5 International Organisation of Standardisation/International Electrotechnical Commission

6 Small and Medium Businesses

This emerging standard, tailored for small-to-medium-sized businesses and not-for-profits in Australia, offers a practical roadmap for Directors. It distils best practice into board-level checklists, capability maturity scales and oversight tools that help Directors assess whether their governance posture is fit-for-purpose.

I've introduced SMB1001:2025 in multiple boardrooms as a bridge between regulatory compliance and practical board oversight. It's become an essential tool in democratising cyber governance, making it accessible to organisations that may not have an in-house security team or enterprise-level budgets.

The bottom line? These frameworks aren't just for ticking boxes. They help Directors understand what 'good' looks like. They provide a shared language between boards and CISOs. And they create a foundation for continuous improvement.

Because cybersecurity governance isn't about perfection – it's about direction. And frameworks give us the compass.

The Cyber Maturity Model: Asking the Right Questions

Boards often ask me, '*How do we know where we stand on cyber?*' My answer: '*Benchmark your maturity – but start with the right questions.*'

This simplified model below is based on my advisory work across industries. It helps Directors reflect not only on their organisation's cyber posture, but also their own readiness to govern it:

Level	Description	Key Board Question
Reactive	Incidents drive action.	'What just happened – and why weren't we ready?'
Compliance	Policies exist, but the impact is unclear.	'Are we ticking boxes, or truly mitigating risk?'
Managed Risk	Cyber linked to risk frameworks.	'How is cyber integrated into our enterprise risk strategy?'
Proactive	Threats are anticipated and rehearsed.	'Are we pressure-testing scenarios and updating our playbooks?'
Resilient	Cyber is part of culture and values.	'Are we cyber-ready, adaptable, and continuously improving?'

This isn't a technology roadmap; it's a governance litmus test. And every board should ask: *Where are we today? Where should we be? And what will it take to close that gap?*

Cyber maturity doesn't come from more tools. It comes from better questions. And those questions start with the board.

Culture Eats Technology for Breakfast

Cyber resilience doesn't start with technology; it starts with mindset. An organisation's ability to withstand and recover from cyber threats depends more on its culture than its code.

Technology can fail. Firewalls can be bypassed. But a culture of vigilance? That's far harder to compromise.

I've advised organisations where the same phishing simulation was run three times, and the staff kept clicking. Not because they were careless, but because cybersecurity was never embedded into the way the business operated. It was treated like a compliance task, not a leadership imperative.

Boards have a unique role to play in shaping cyber culture:

- **Prioritise Cybersecurity:** If Directors treat cybersecurity as a strategic priority, so will the executive and staff.
- **Insist on training:** Not just for frontline staff, but for Directors too. Cyber awareness training should be an annual requirement for the board, not because regulators demand it, but because good governance does.
- **Conduct tabletop exercises:** Nothing focuses the mind like a simulated crisis. Rehearse your breach response as you would a financial or reputational crisis.
- **Review response plans:** Ensure incident response and crisis communication plans are current, tested and understood across leadership.

- **Integrate cyber into enterprise risk management:** Cyber shouldn't be siloed. It should be integrated into the organisation's overall risk approach.

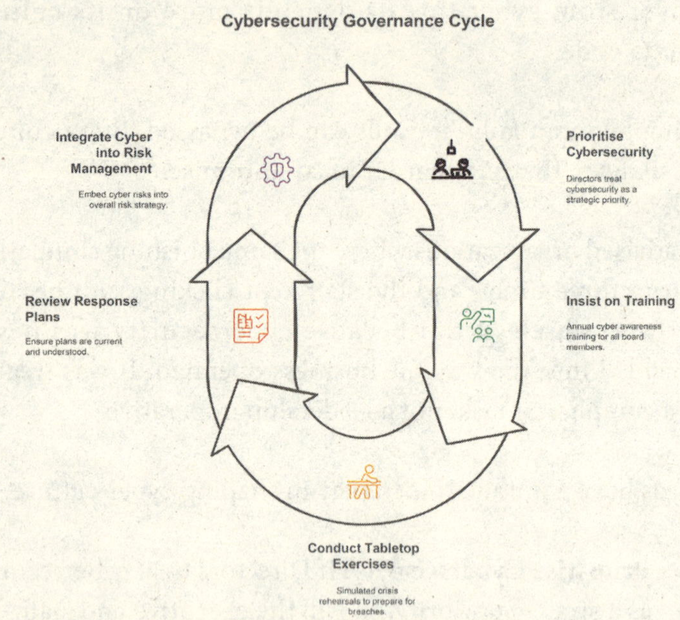

One of the most impactful governance shifts I've seen is when cybersecurity becomes a standing item at every board meeting, not just when something goes wrong. Boards that talk about cyber regularly tend to act on it decisively.

Cybersecurity is not an IT behaviour – it's a leadership behaviour. And like all leadership behaviours, it's contagious.

If the culture in your organisation doesn't prioritise cyber, no tool will save you. But if it does, you're already halfway to resilience.

The Cost of Complacency Is Rising

A breach doesn't just cost money. It costs reputation, trust, opportunity, and, for Directors, sometimes careers.

In the aftermath of the 2022 Optus and Medibank breaches, two of the most high-profile cyberattacks in Australian corporate history, we saw not just regulatory scrutiny but public outcry. Customers were furious. Class actions followed. And confidence in leadership was shaken.

In the Optus case, the CEO resigned. In Medibank's situation, the reputational hit was profound, with ongoing fallout as investigations and litigations unfolded. Latitude and Medisecure have also made headlines, reinforcing one harsh reality: even well-established organisations can find themselves exposed and their boards under pressure.

Internationally, the Uber case sent shockwaves through governance circles. The company's former CSO was convicted of covering up a data breach. And in other global cases, from Target to Equifax, board-level failures in cyber oversight led to resignations, financial losses and regulatory fines running into hundreds of millions.

Consequences of inaction:

- ASIC investigations into Director liability.
- Class actions by shareholders and customers.
- Criminal sanctions in the event of gross negligence.

- Loss of market confidence and share price declines.
- Disqualification from future board roles.

Cybersecurity is no longer an invisible risk; it's a career-defining one. Directors must ask themselves: in the wake of a breach, could I confidently explain what I did to mitigate cyber risk? If the answer isn't yes, then the cost of complacency may be higher than you think.

Final Thoughts: Secure Your Legacy

If you take one thing from this chapter, let it be this: cybersecurity is not an IT issue. It is a governance issue. The board must own it, resource it, challenge it and embed it – just like any other critical enterprise risk.

As someone who has served on boards and advised them across sectors, I know this work isn't easy. But it is essential. Cybersecurity is no longer about ticking boxes; it's about protecting your organisation's mission, reputation and future viability.

So, let's start with a simple commitment. As Directors, we must challenge ourselves to:

- Make cybersecurity a standing agenda item at every board meeting, not just when a breach occurs.
- Demand clarity from CISOs, CIOs and risk officers, not just comfort.

- Invest in continuous learning, not because a regulator demands it, but because our responsibility demands it.

In the pages ahead, I'll show you how to:

- Identify your organisation's true cyber risk exposure.
- Engage with your CIO and CISO meaningfully.
- Integrate cybersecurity into strategic and financial planning.
- Build board-level resilience frameworks.
- Fulfil your duties with confidence and clarity.

Cyber threats aren't going away, but with the right knowledge and leadership, your board can be part of the solution, not the next headline.

Because cybersecurity is no longer a technical obligation. It's a boardroom responsibility.

And it's time we treated it like one.

CHAPTER 2

Drowning in Tech Speak? Here's Cyber Risk in Plain English

LET'S FACE IT, CYBERSECURITY CAN feel like a tangled web of acronyms, jargon and fast-moving threats. For many Board Directors, it's an area that feels abstract, highly technical and often overwhelming. But here's the good news: your role on the board isn't to become a cyber expert – it's to become cyber literate. And that starts with understanding cyber risk in plain English.

This chapter is designed to remove the fog. Whether you're leading a large ASX-listed company or a lean not-for-profit governed by community trust, the cybersecurity risks are real, and they're rising. As Directors, your responsibility is not to learn how firewalls or multi-factor authentication work, but to grasp how cyber threats can affect your organisation's strategic objectives, disrupt operations and erode stakeholder confidence.

The AICD[7] is clear on this point: boards have a fiduciary obligation to oversee enterprise risk, and that includes cyber risk. Cybersecurity governance is no longer a matter for the IT team alone; it's a board-level priority that must be integrated into the organisation's risk management frameworks.

The AICD's Cyber Security Governance Principles make it clear:

Cybersecurity must be aligned with your business objectives and overall risk appetite.

- Directors should receive regular reporting on the organisation's cybersecurity posture.
- Boards must promote a culture where cyber resilience is seen as a strategic issue, not just a technical one.
- All organisations must comply with relevant laws, such as the NDB[8] scheme under the Privacy Act 1988 (Cth).

For Directors in APRA-regulated entities such as financial services and insurance, this is further reinforced by Prudential Standard CPS 234, which outlines explicit expectations for governance, incident response and assurance of information

7 Australian Institute of Company Directors

8 Notifiable Data Breaches

security capabilities. Boards must not only ask the right questions, but they must ensure the answers are meaningful, measurable, and risk-aligned.

Now let's talk about not-for-profits. The ACNC[9] is increasingly attentive to how NFPs manage data and digital risks. While NFPs may not face the same commercial pressure as listed entities, they shoulder an equally heavy burden – public trust. As a Director of an NFP, you're responsible for stewarding donor information, member records and community reputation.

The ACNC expects:

- Implementation of sensible, fit-for-purpose cybersecurity controls.
- Compliance with Australian privacy laws and breach notification requirements.
- A clear risk management strategy that includes ongoing cyber awareness and training across staff, volunteers and leadership.

It's easy to assume that cyber risk is 'less relevant' for NFPs or smaller organisations, but that assumption is dangerous. Cybercriminals often view these entities as soft targets–underfunded, underprepared and under-protected. A successful attack on a small charity can be just as devastating, perhaps more so, than one on a listed company.

---

9 Australian Charities and Not-for-profits Commission

Across all sectors, the story is the same: cyber risk is not about bits and bytes, it's about business continuity, financial health, legal exposure and reputation. The role of the board is to ensure these risks are governed just as rigorously as any other critical area of enterprise risk.

That includes:

- Ensuring that the right questions are being asked at board meetings.
- Demanding visibility into how cyber risks are being prioritised and mitigated.
- Championing a culture of security awareness from the top down.

Think of cyber risk not as an IT function but as a modern-day corporate hygiene issue. Just as financial audits or WHS compliance are non-negotiable, cyber resilience must be approached with the same diligence. The threat landscape is evolving – and it's unforgiving.

We've already seen how real this can get. Consider the 2022 Optus data breach, where over 10 million Australians had their personal data compromised, including passport and Medicare numbers. The fallout wasn't just technical; it triggered class actions, political scrutiny and long-term reputational damage. The boardroom was thrust into the spotlight. Or take the Medibank breach, where sensitive health records were stolen and publicly leaked. The questions being asked weren't about firewalls – they were about how the board had exercised its duty of care.

These are cautionary tales, but they're also valuable learning moments. They remind us that the responsibility to ask the right questions, to fund the right capabilities, and to challenge the status quo sits squarely with the board.

The threat landscape is evolving. So must the boardroom conversation. And it starts with clarity. In this chapter, we will decode what cyber risk really means, why it matters, and how you, as a Board Director, can lead your organisation through this terrain with confidence and clarity.

Because at the end of the day, cybersecurity isn't just about protecting data. It's about protecting trust, and trust is a board-level issue.

What Exactly is Cyber Risk?

Let's break this down. Cyber risk is not just about hackers trying to break into your systems. It's about the potential business consequences that follow if they succeed. Think of cyber risk like you would think about financial risk or legal liability. It's a form of enterprise risk that can result in financial loss, reputational damage, operational disruption or regulatory penalties if not properly understood and managed.

In plain terms, cyber risk is the likelihood that your organisation will suffer harm because of a failure in technology, people or processes. These failures could come from external threats like ransomware gangs, internal mistakes like sending sensitive data to the wrong person or third-party vendors whose poor security controls expose your systems to danger. It is not just the IT department's job to worry about cyber risk. If a breach occurs and it impacts your customers, shareholders or the continuity of your services, the accountability stops with the board.

Take the Optus breach, for example. The fallout wasn't simply about the data; it was about the erosion of trust. Headlines didn't point fingers at the IT team; they questioned board oversight. The same happened with Medibank. As a Director, when cyber risk is realised, it is your risk to own. So, what does this mean for you?

Cyber risk is dynamic. It evolves. And it's not going away. The rise in digitisation, remote work, data dependency and cloud-based infrastructure means there are more opportunities and entry points for cyber threats than ever before. You must ask: how prepared is your organisation?

To give you a clearer framework, cybersecurity risk typically affects three key areas, referred to as the CIA triad:

- **Confidentiality**: Are we protecting sensitive data from unauthorised access?
- **Integrity**: Can we trust that our data and systems haven't been tampered with?
- **Availability**: Are our critical services and systems accessible when needed?

If any of these pillars are compromised, the consequences can be significant.

Now let's layer this with a few examples:

- If an attacker encrypts your data and holds it ransom (ransomware), that's a threat to availability.
- If a staff member accidentally emails a customer file to the wrong person, that's a breach of confidentiality.
- If a malicious actor alters financial reporting data, that's a compromise of integrity.

For boards, the question is no longer '*What is cyber risk?*', it's '*Are we governing this risk with the same rigour we apply to financial, operational and legal risk?*'

Cyber risk is a business risk. And like any business risk, it demands visibility, resources and strategy at the board level. In the next section, we'll explore why this matters so deeply—and why the boardroom needs to own the cyber conversation.

Why Cyber Risk Matters to the Board

Let's be clear – cyber risk is no longer a hypothetical 'what if'. It's a 'when', and increasingly, a 'what now?' scenario. Whether you're sitting on the board of an ASX-listed enterprise or a not-for-profit serving local communities, cyber threats can reach your doorstep with little warning and devastating consequences.

As Board Directors, your duty is not to configure firewalls or decode security logs. Your responsibility is to understand the strategic, operational and reputational impact of a cyber incident, and to ensure the organisation is prepared, protected and resilient.

It's Not Just About Technology, It's About Trust

Cybersecurity isn't about the blinking lights in a data centre. It's about protecting the trust your stakeholders place in you. Customers trust you with their personal information. Donors trust you with their money. Regulators trust you to meet your obligations. One breach can undermine all of that.

When Medibank suffered a cyberattack in 2022, over 9.7 million current and former customers had their data exposed. This wasn't just a privacy failure; it became a public reckoning on governance. The attack raised pressing questions: had the board understood the organisation's cyber risk exposure? Were investments in cyber maturity sufficient? Had risk scenarios been rehearsed? These are governance-level questions, not IT queries.

Cyber risk is not just a tech issue – it's a leadership issue. A breach is not just an IT failure; it's a breakdown in trust, governance and accountability. It cuts to the heart of your organisation's integrity.

And this is especially true in the not-for-profit space. Many NFPs handle deeply personal data – medical histories, family backgrounds and financial vulnerabilities. A cyber incident in this context doesn't just breach systems, it breaches human dignity.

As a Director, if your organisation is entrusted with sensitive data such as health records, financials and identity documents, then you are a steward of that data. That's a weighty responsibility. And it's one that cannot be outsourced.

Trust is built over time, but lost in a moment. And in a digital-first world, where stakeholders are acutely sensitive to data privacy and ethics, your organisation's licence to operate hinges on its ability to safeguard that trust.

The board's role is to ensure that trust is baked into your governance, risk and strategy frameworks. That means:

- Championing a culture where trust and security go hand in hand.
- Treating data protection as a core leadership issue, not an IT line item.
- Ensuring cyber risk is considered in strategic planning, not just compliance.

Because ultimately, your cybersecurity posture isn't just a reflection of your technology – it's a reflection of your values.

Cyber Incidents Impact the Bottom Line

Still tempted to view cyber risk as an operational detail? Let's look at the numbers.

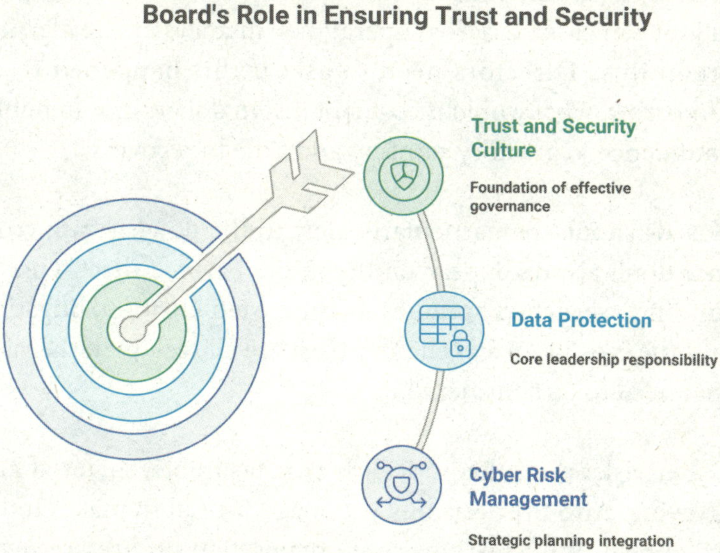

According to IBM's Cost of a Data Breach Report (2023), the average cost of a data breach in Australia is over AUD $4 million. This includes legal costs, forensic investigations, crisis communications, regulatory fines and long-term reputational harm. And that's for one incident.

For not-for-profits, the impact is even more acute. A single breach could compromise donor databases, disrupt community programs and see funding pulled. Unlike large corporations, many NFPs lack the financial cushion to absorb this kind of shock. That makes resilience not just a strategy, but a survival imperative.

This is not just a technology issue, it's a bottom-line one. Whether it's a ransomware attack locking up mission-critical systems or an insider mistake exposing confidential data, the fallout can cascade across operations, finances and leadership credibility. Directors need to ask: if this happened to us tomorrow, what would it cost, not just in dollars, but in public confidence, regulatory scrutiny and time to recover?

Boards should be particularly alert to the downstream costs that don't always appear on the initial balance sheet. Loss of funding, weakened brand reputation, staff attrition, litigation and the erosion of stakeholder trust are all real, material risks that need to be considered.

Cyber risk is not theoretical. It is measurable, material and growing. And the decisions you make (or fail to make) today will directly influence how your organisation survives, recovers or falls behind tomorrow.

Directors are Now on the Regulatory Radar

Here's what's different now: regulators are no longer just targeting the entity; they're looking at the role of Directors.

ASIC has been increasingly vocal about governance failures in the aftermath of cyber incidents. In fact, it has signalled its intent to take enforcement action where boards fail to meet their obligations. We've already seen this play out in enforcement investigations following breaches where regulators examined not just technical faults, but governance gaps. The message is clear: 'We won't just be asking what your IT team did. We'll be asking what the board knew – and when.'

Prudential Standard CPS 234 from APRA makes board accountability explicit for regulated entities. It mandates that Directors ensure information security capabilities are both fit-for-purpose and regularly tested for effectiveness. This isn't a one-off audit; it's an ongoing obligation tied directly to board oversight.

And the ACNC isn't far behind. It expects NFP Boards to treat cyber risk as part of their core governance duties, especially where sensitive beneficiary or donor data is involved. It's not enough to say, 'We're small' or 'We outsource IT'. The expectation is that even community-run organisations have asked the right questions, ensured suitable protections and are prepared to respond if things go wrong.

What does this mean for you as a Director? It means plausible deniability is no longer a shield. Directors must demonstrate active engagement with cyber risk through governance structures, investment decisions and ongoing boardroom dialogue.

This is where the AICD's guidance becomes essential. It calls on all Directors, regardless of sector, to be cyber-literate, to engage in ongoing education, and to challenge management on how risks are being identified, prioritised and treated.

Asking questions like:

- Are we satisfied with the level of cyber maturity in the organisation?

- Have we tested our incident response plan in a simulated exercise?
- How are cyber risks being reported to the board – and are those metrics meaningful?

These aren't technical questions. They're governance questions. And asking them isn't just best practice – it's expected.

As cyber threats continue to make headlines, the spotlight on Directors will only intensify. Regulatory expectations are shifting from reactive to proactive oversight. The time to engage is now. Because when a breach happens (and it likely will), the question won't be '*Did the IT team respond fast enough?*' It will be, '*Did the board do enough to prevent it?*'

Cyber Risk Demands Governance, Not Just IT Controls

Managing cyber risk is not about having the best antivirus software. It's about board-level governance.

That means ensuring that:

- Cyber risk is a standing agenda item at risk and audit committees
- The board understands the organisation's current cyber maturity and risk exposure
- There is a tested incident response plan, and the board knows its role in a crisis
- Funding for cybersecurity aligns with the risk appetite and business priorities.

Let's not forget third-party risk. Many recent breaches, including the Latitude Financial breach in 2023, were initiated via vendors. If your supply chain includes software providers, cloud hosts or outsourced services, their risks are your risks. As a board, you need oversight of these dependencies.

Cyber governance also means asking: How often are our third-party vendors audited for cybersecurity compliance? Are they contractually obligated to notify us of incidents? Is there a clear owner internally who manages third-party cyber risk? This is where governance comes into play. It's not just about policies and tools, it's about establishing clear accountabilities, ensuring information flows to the board and embedding cyber into business-as-usual decision-making.

Directors should be confident that cyber risk isn't just managed reactively, it's governed strategically. The difference? A reactive approach waits for an incident. A governance-led approach anticipates it, plans for it and tests the organisation's readiness. Because in today's environment, the question is not whether your organisation will face a cyber event. It's when. And the quality of governance will define the quality of the response.

Final Thoughts: Why It Matters to You, As a Director

You're not being asked to become a cybersecurity expert. But you are expected to ask the right questions, and to recognise when the answers don't add up. Your leadership sets the tone. If cyber is treated as a low-priority technical issue, that attitude will cascade through the organisation. But if the board demonstrates visible ownership of cyber risk, it signals to management, staff and external stakeholders that this is a critical area of governance.

Ultimately, the question is simple: If a breach occurred tomorrow, would you be confident that your organisation could respond swiftly, recover safely and maintain the trust of those it serves? If the answer is anything less than a resounding 'yes', then this book is your roadmap to lifting that confidence.

Because cybersecurity isn't just a matter of risk management, it's a test of leadership. And the board sets the standard.

CHAPTER 3

Cybersecurity ROI: Is It Just a Myth?

IN MODERN BUSINESS, ROI[10] IS an indispensable metric that Directors use daily to measure success. Yet, when cybersecurity enters the boardroom discussion, ROI presents a paradox. Traditional investments such as new product launches or market expansions yield clear, measurable financial outcomes. In stark contrast, cybersecurity investments often provide intangible yet critical outcomes: reducing risk exposure, ensuring compliance and safeguarding the company's reputation.

These benefits, although crucial, do not neatly fit into conventional financial metrics, thus complicating board-level decision-making processes, especially within Australian businesses facing an increasingly complex cyber threat environment.

10 Return on investment

As Australian Directors, we are acutely aware of the growing cyber threat facing our organisations. The ACSC[11] reported more than 67,500 cybersecurity incidents in 2021 alone, a sobering reality highlighting the relentless assault on our business infrastructures. Yet, despite these staggering numbers, convincing stakeholders to approve substantial cybersecurity budgets remains challenging.

The conundrum is clear: cybersecurity's most significant victories are often invisible, measured only by the absence of attacks and incidents. From my experience advising boards and as a former CIO responsible for large-scale cybersecurity programs, I've observed firsthand how difficult it is to articulate cybersecurity's value to stakeholders accustomed to more tangible returns. Consider cybersecurity as preventive medicine – essential, yet the measure of its success is often what doesn't occur.

Just as one might question the investment in preventive healthcare until faced with illness, cybersecurity investments often come under scrutiny precisely because their effectiveness is demonstrated quietly and proactively behind the scenes.

This paradox becomes especially evident during high-profile incidents, such as the Medibank data breach in 2022. This incident vividly demonstrated the severe financial and reputational consequences that arise when cybersecurity infrastructure is insufficiently funded or undervalued. Despite clear warnings, Medibank, like many organisations, faced

11 Australian Cyber Security Centre

considerable remediation costs, regulatory fines and irreparable harm to customer trust. This breach underscored the reality that Directors must confront: the cost of cybersecurity may appear significant upfront, but it pales in comparison to the price of inadequate protection.

To effectively engage with this paradox, Directors must adopt a broader, more strategic view of cybersecurity. This chapter will unpack why traditional ROI measures fall short when evaluating cybersecurity, exploring practical ways for Australian businesses to measure the intangible yet critical returns of their cybersecurity investments. By reframing cybersecurity spending as strategic business investments rather than mere technical expenses, we can better articulate and appreciate its profound yet often invisible value, enabling clearer boardroom discussions and more informed decision-making.

Together, we will navigate this nuanced debate, combining insights from frameworks such as ISO27001, SMB1001:2025 and NIST with practical, real-world examples from the Australian business landscape. My goal is to empower you, as Directors, with the knowledge and tools needed to articulate a compelling case for cybersecurity investment, transforming it from a murky topic into a clear strategic imperative essential for safeguarding your organisation's future.

Why Australian Businesses Struggle to See the ROI

Australian businesses have historically grappled with understanding and justifying the ROI of cybersecurity investments, largely due to their perception as purely an IT issue. For decades, cybersecurity was compartmentalised within IT departments, tasked primarily with basic malware and virus prevention. This limited viewpoint created a pervasive disconnect, leading many Directors and executives to perceive cybersecurity spending merely as operational costs rather than strategic investments.

From my experience both as a CIO and a Board Advisor, I have witnessed how this misalignment fosters significant resistance to allocating adequate cybersecurity budgets. The common sentiment among leadership has often been, '*If it isn't broken, why invest heavily to fix it*?' Yet, as cyber threats have evolved dramatically, becoming sophisticated, targeted and financially devastating, the role of cybersecurity has extended beyond IT, penetrating deeply into core business strategy and operations.

A recent report by the AICD[12] highlighted that nearly 60% of Australian boards recognise cybersecurity as a critical business risk, yet astonishingly, most admit to lacking a comprehensive, integrated strategy to address it. Cybersecurity frequently remains trapped within IT budgets, isolated from broader business planning and strategic risk discussions. Consequently, its true value and strategic importance are undervalued and poorly articulated in financial terms.

One fundamental issue is the indirect and long-term nature of cybersecurity's ROI. Unlike conventional investments, such as new software systems or marketing initiatives, cybersecurity's

12 Australian Institute of Company Directors

successes often remain invisible until disaster is prevented. For example, the returns from network monitoring, penetration testing or employee awareness training materialise quietly, behind the scenes, only becoming visibly evident when threats are neutralised before causing damage. This indirect nature complicates justifications for large-scale investments, particularly among Australian executives accustomed to precise, immediate performance metrics.

The Medibank data breach in 2022 provides a sobering illustration of this point. Despite previous underinvestment due to ROI scepticism, the breach's aftermath starkly revealed the true cost of inadequate cybersecurity. Medibank incurred millions in customer notifications, regulatory penalties, remediation efforts, and perhaps most significantly, irreparable damage to its brand reputation. This incident exemplifies the hidden, but critical value of cybersecurity – the immeasurable cost avoided through strategic prevention.

To address this persistent challenge, Directors must reposition cybersecurity within their strategic framework. It requires shifting the mindset from viewing cybersecurity as an expense toward recognising it as a proactive investment in risk management and business resilience.

Adopting robust cybersecurity frameworks such as ISO27001, SMB1001:2025, or leveraging insights from NIST guidelines can assist in demonstrating this broader value to stakeholders. By embracing this strategic alignment, boards can better comprehend and articulate cybersecurity's ROI, thereby ensuring adequate investment and fortifying their organisations against the increasingly complex and dangerous cyber landscape.

The Growing Cyber Threat Landscape

As Directors, it's imperative that we grasp the rapidly evolving cyber threat landscape confronting Australian businesses. Each year, cyber threats become not only more prevalent but increasingly sophisticated, requiring heightened vigilance and strategic preparedness. The ACSC[13] confirmed that in 2021, Australian businesses faced a record volume of targeted cyberattacks, marking a disturbing upward trend.

One of the most critical and immediate threats facing Australian organisations today is ransomware. Between 2020 and 2021, ransomware attacks surged by 15%, highlighting a significant escalation in both frequency and severity. High-profile incidents involving well-known Australian brands such as Latitude Financial and Channel Nine underscore how even sophisticated businesses can fall victim. These attacks disrupt business continuity, inflict substantial financial losses and severely damage organisational reputation. Directors must understand that when faced with ransomware, companies often confront a stark decision: pay a costly ransom, risking regulatory scrutiny and reputational fallout, or refuse and potentially suffer prolonged operational disruption and irrecoverable data loss.

---

13 Australian Cyber Security Centre

Phishing attacks present another considerable challenge to Australian businesses. According to Proofpoint's 2021 report, an alarming 85% of Australian organisations experienced phishing attempts within a single year. These attacks capitalise on employee vulnerability, tricking individuals into unwittingly disclosing sensitive information or inadvertently downloading malware. From my experience, many breaches result from simple human errors, avoidable scenarios that underscore the critical need for robust employee training programs and comprehensive cybersecurity awareness initiatives. Proactively investing in employee education around cybersecurity hygiene is no longer optional; it's an essential defence mechanism for businesses.

The COVID-19 pandemic accelerated the shift to remote working, introducing new cybersecurity vulnerabilities previously unseen. Australian businesses rapidly transitioning to remote setups without proportionate cybersecurity measures found themselves increasingly susceptible to cyber threats. Issues such as insecure remote access points, outdated software, insufficient training and unsecured home networks created fertile grounds for exploitation by cybercriminals. The rapid digital transformation triggered by remote work mandates highlighted a gap between existing cybersecurity protocols and emerging operational realities.

Directors should also consider the broader financial implications associated with cybersecurity breaches. The Australian Cybersecurity Business Sector Report (2020) cited the average cost of a data breach incident as $276,000, yet this figure captures only immediate financial impacts. True costs often extend beyond immediate financial losses to include legal expenses, regulatory penalties, prolonged operational downtime and long-term reputational damage. For businesses, these hidden and enduring costs can prove catastrophic, severely undermining shareholder value and stakeholder trust.

As Directors, comprehensively understanding these evolving cyber threats is essential for strategic decision-making around cybersecurity investments. By recognising these risks, boards can make informed, proactive investments in cybersecurity initiatives such as threat intelligence, continuous employee education and advanced security monitoring systems. Such proactive measures yield substantial indirect returns by significantly reducing the likelihood and impact of breaches, thereby safeguarding the business's long-term viability.

My experience advising boards and working across diverse sectors has consistently demonstrated the importance of embedding cybersecurity within the organisation's strategic fabric. Cyber threats are dynamic; thus, our response must be equally agile and forward-looking. Leveraging proven cybersecurity frameworks such as ISO27001, SMB1001:2025 and NIST, alongside robust risk management processes, empowers Directors to quantify cybersecurity's value effectively. This strategic approach positions cybersecurity not merely as a defensive tactic but as a critical enabler of organisational resilience and competitive advantage.

Understanding the magnitude and intricacy of today's cyber threat landscape is pivotal for Directors. Recognising cybersecurity threats as strategic business risks and proactively addressing these challenges positions businesses to thrive amid an increasingly volatile digital environment. The key to effectively navigating this landscape lies in shifting our perception of cybersecurity from reactive cost containment to proactive, strategic investment, essential for safeguarding not just IT infrastructure but the long-term health and prosperity of our businesses.

Cybersecurity ROI: Strategic Investments Beyond the Balance Sheet

In addressing cybersecurity at the board level, we must recognise that the value extends far beyond traditional financial metrics. While ROI typically revolves around numbers and tangible returns, cybersecurity investments deliver substantial strategic value, encompassing risk management, compliance, customer trust and business continuity. As Directors, we need to shift our mindset to embrace a broader, strategic perspective – seeing cybersecurity not merely as an operational expenditure but as a critical business enabler.

One of the most compelling yet overlooked aspects of cybersecurity ROI is risk reduction. Investing strategically in cybersecurity substantially mitigates risks, such as data breaches, system outages and long-term reputational damage. Consider the global impact of the 2017 WannaCry ransomware attack, which incurred over $4 billion in damages worldwide. Here in Australia, entities across government, healthcare and the private sector experienced significant disruptions. Strategic investments in proactive cybersecurity practices, such as robust threat intelligence and comprehensive employee awareness training, directly reduce the probability and severity of such incidents, safeguarding organisational resilience.

Furthermore, robust cybersecurity frameworks support businesses in meeting critical compliance standards. The APPs[14], embedded within the Privacy Act 1988, mandate

---

14 Australian Privacy Principles

mandates stringent protections for personal data. Non-compliance exposes businesses not only to substantial financial penalties (up to $2.1 million), but also to lasting reputational harm. By proactively embedding cybersecurity compliance measures, businesses significantly reduce their regulatory risks and demonstrate accountability, reinforcing stakeholder confidence.

The reputational implications of cybersecurity cannot be overstated. As consumer awareness around data privacy increases, organisations that actively demonstrate robust cybersecurity measures, secure significant competitive advantages. For instance, Australian financial institutions, such as the Commonwealth Bank and ANZ have leveraged their cybersecurity commitments to boost customer confidence and enhance market reputation. Conversely, businesses that underestimate cybersecurity risks risk severe reputational fallout and potential customer attrition after breaches.

Another strategic benefit of cybersecurity investment is enhanced business continuity. In sectors where downtime equates directly to significant financial losses, such as finance, healthcare, and telecommunications, continuity is critical. Effective cybersecurity strategies not only reduce vulnerabilities but also enable swift recovery and minimal downtime when incidents occur. Directors must view cybersecurity as integral to maintaining ongoing operations rather than a standalone IT responsibility.

To effectively advocate for cybersecurity investments, Directors must communicate clearly the direct and indirect returns to stakeholders. Illustrating potential cost savings from proactive investments versus reactive responses can be particularly persuasive. Consider an Australian retailer investing proactively in cybersecurity. Regular software updates, network monitoring and targeted employee training could help avoid a significant data breach and its associated fallout, including regulatory penalties, legal fees and lost revenue.

Moreover, leveraging case studies can strengthen the boardroom narrative around cybersecurity. For instance, Australian telecommunications providers effectively mitigate the growing threat of DDoS[15] attacks through proactive cybersecurity investments. Highlighting such real-world scenarios clarifies how cybersecurity expenditure directly contributes to organisational resilience, operational stability, and competitive positioning.

In my experience advising boards across diverse industries, I've consistently observed that businesses adopting a strategic, forward-looking cybersecurity approach gain long-term competitive advantages. Utilising proven frameworks such as ISO27001, SMB1001:2025, and NIST enables boards to clearly measure and articulate cybersecurity's strategic value, aligning these investments with broader organisational objectives.

Ultimately, Directors must advocate for a strategic approach, viewing cybersecurity as an investment with measurable, yet often indirect returns that extend beyond immediate financial considerations. By doing so, we not only safeguard

---

15 Distributed Denial of Service

our organisations from cyber threats but also position them strategically for sustainable growth and resilience in a digital-first world.

Final Thoughts: Shifting the Narrative

The cybersecurity ROI debate is evolving as Australian businesses increasingly recognise cybersecurity as essential to their strategic framework. The traditional reliance on clear, immediate financial metrics has proven insufficient in accurately capturing cybersecurity's true value. Directors must now embrace the reality that cybersecurity investments transcend conventional financial returns, safeguarding the business from long-term reputational damage, significant regulatory fines, legal liabilities and substantial operational disruptions.

Changing the narrative from viewing cybersecurity merely as an IT cost to a critical strategic investment is vital. From my extensive experience advising boards, I've observed that organisations most effectively protected from cyber threats are those whose Directors proactively integrate cybersecurity within their broader business strategies. Directors must actively champion this mindset shift, reframing cybersecurity from an expense line item to a core pillar of corporate risk management, business continuity planning and competitive differentiation.

To foster this transition, Directors should begin with practical actions such as embedding cybersecurity discussions into regular board agendas, ensuring continuous oversight rather than episodic reviews. Utilising established frameworks such as ISO27001, SMB1001:2025, NIST, and cybersecurity maturity models provides clear benchmarks and progress indicators that align cybersecurity efforts with broader strategic objectives. Directors should also prioritise cybersecurity literacy, not necessarily technical proficiency, empowering themselves to ask informed questions and make confident decisions regarding cybersecurity investments.

Real-world scenarios and case studies should regularly be discussed within board meetings to provide tangible illustrations of both successful cybersecurity investments and cautionary tales from breaches. These narratives can effectively highlight cybersecurity's strategic importance and help boards appreciate the significant, albeit often intangible, returns on investment.

Ultimately, as Directors, we have a responsibility to elevate cybersecurity within our organisations, ensuring it receives the strategic priority and investment necessary for safeguarding long-term business resilience and success. The clear truth emerging from ongoing cyber incidents across Australian businesses is straightforward: investing proactively in cybersecurity isn't merely prudent, it's essential for sustainable business growth and protection in today's digitally connected economy.

CHAPTER 4

The Missing Link in Your Board's Risk Strategy: Cybersecurity Governance

IN AN INCREASINGLY DIGITAL-FIRST LANDSCAPE, cybersecurity governance has emerged as an indispensable component of robust corporate risk management. For Boards of Directors, taking a proactive stance in shaping and overseeing an organisation's cybersecurity strategy is no longer optional; it is an essential fiduciary responsibility. Recent high-profile data breaches, such as the Optus incident in 2022, where nearly 10 million customer records were compromised, and Latitude's massive breach affecting over 14 million customers, underline the stark reality that cybersecurity risks transcend technical departments and impact the entire enterprise.

Cyberattacks are becoming alarmingly frequent and sophisticated, directly impacting operational continuity, financial stability and corporate reputation. The 2019 Canva breach, which exposed the personal data of 137 million users, and the highly targeted ransomware attack on Medibank in 2022, demonstrate clearly that cyber risk management must feature prominently on every board's agenda. It is not merely a question of compliance but strategic survival.

Boards must recognise that cybersecurity governance extends beyond technical management – it is a strategic business imperative that requires thoughtful oversight, clear accountability and active engagement at the highest levels. My extensive experience, both as a CIO and Board Advisor, has repeatedly shown that effective governance occurs when Directors shift their perspective from cybersecurity as a purely technical issue to viewing it through the lens of overall business risk and resilience.

In this chapter, you will gain practical insights and a structured governance framework that empowers you as Board Directors to embed cybersecurity effectively into your organisation's strategic fabric. From clearly defining your governance role and constructing resilient cybersecurity strategies to fostering meaningful dialogue with your Chief Information Security Officer and senior leadership, this section provides actionable guidance for Directors committed to robust cybersecurity governance.

Additionally, the AICD[16] provides resources on their website or through their member portal, which can serve as valuable reference points to assist you in confidently navigating and leading cybersecurity discussions and decisions.

---

16 Australian Institute of Company Directors

Through informed governance, you can not only mitigate cyber risks but also position your organisation to respond swiftly and effectively, safeguarding trust and ensuring long-term organisational resilience.

The Role of the Board in Cybersecurity Governance

As Directors, our role has always been to steer our organisations towards sustainable success. Cybersecurity governance aligns seamlessly with this strategic responsibility. However, a persistent challenge remains: the gap between board-level awareness of cybersecurity risks and the practical oversight necessary to manage these threats effectively.

Too often, cybersecurity is mistakenly viewed solely as an IT issue; however, cybersecurity is fundamentally a business issue. It influences operations, finance, reputation and ultimately, shareholder value. High-profile breaches, such as those at Optus and Medibank, have vividly demonstrated the broader implications of failing to prioritise cybersecurity at the strategic level.

As Directors, it's crucial we recognise that cybersecurity governance isn't just about technical defences—it's about cultivating a resilient culture across our entire organisation, from senior leadership right down to frontline teams. The board must champion this culture, ensuring readiness not just to prevent incidents but to respond swiftly and recover effectively when cyber incidents inevitably occur.

Our primary responsibility as board members is to ensure organisational resilience. To achieve this, we must possess a clear, thorough understanding of our cybersecurity posture, including the specific risks we face. We must engage confidently with our CISOs, asking informed, strategic questions to ensure our cybersecurity initiatives are not only technically robust but also aligned closely with our broader business objectives.

In short, cybersecurity governance requires active, informed and decisive leadership. It's not merely about managing risk; it's about leveraging cybersecurity as a strategic asset to secure long-term success and trust in an increasingly digital world.

Cybersecurity Governance Framework

A robust cybersecurity governance framework is foundational for effective oversight and management of cybersecurity risks. In my experience advising boards, I've observed that the most successful frameworks are built upon three core pillars: leadership and accountability, proactive risk management and continuous improvement.

I. Leadership and Accountability:

- **CISO leadership**:

  Your CISO[17] is more than just a technical expert; they are a strategic partner for your board. Establishing clear, open communication lines with your CISO ensures you stay informed with actionable insights into your

17 Chief Information Security Officer

cybersecurity posture. Embrace and empower their role as your principal cybersecurity advisor.

- **Board oversight:**

  Your oversight as a board is vital. Cybersecurity decisions must be embedded within broader strategic discussions. Ensure your CISO has adequate resources and clear authority to implement security measures. Cybersecurity considerations must become integral to every major business decision.

II. Risk Management:

- **Cybersecurity Risk Assessment:**

  Begin with an honest and comprehensive risk assessment. You must understand the exact threats your organisation faces, be it ransomware, phishing attacks or data breaches. Regularly revisit this assessment to adapt swiftly to the evolving cyber landscape, ensuring preparedness rather than reactivity.

- **Mitigation Strategies**:

  Mitigation strategies should be both robust and holistic. Beyond firewalls and encryption, consider comprehensive policies around access control, staff training, vendor risk management and effective incident response plans. Remember, technology alone is not enough; the human factor is critical.

III. Continuous Improvement:

- **Metrics and Reporting:**

  Demand regular, strategic reports on cybersecurity effectiveness, emphasising outcomes over technical jargon. These reports should clearly articulate cybersecurity's business impact, enabling informed, strategic decision-making.

- **Lessons Learned**:

  Cultivate a culture of continual learning and agility. Adapt quickly from past incidents and emerging threats, staying informed about cutting-edge cybersecurity trends. Continuous improvement isn't optional—it's critical for sustained resilience and success in a digital world.

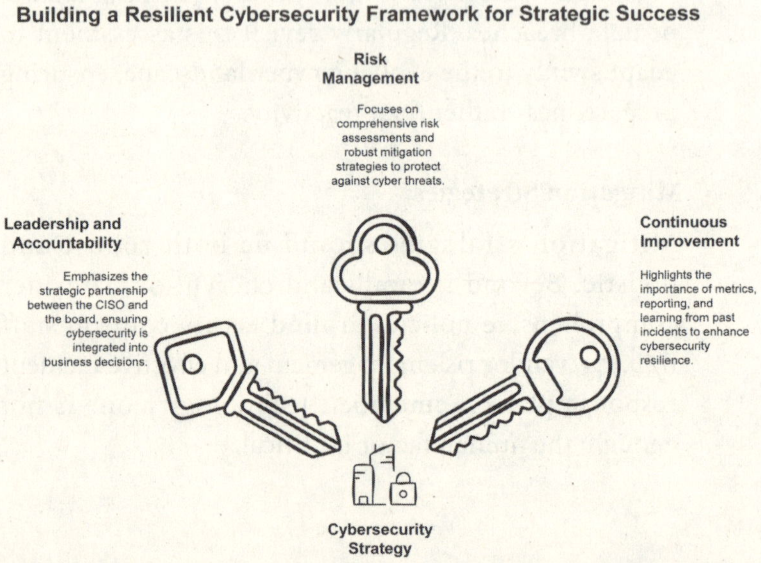

Engagement with the CISO and Other Key Players

One of the most vital yet often underestimated relationships in cybersecurity governance is the one between the board and the CISO. Having served as a CISO for large government organisations, I can personally attest that this partnership is critical. Too frequently, boards only engage superficially with their CISOs during formal presentations, leaving significant gaps in understanding and strategic alignment.

Directors must appreciate that the CISO's role is not merely technical; it is inherently strategic. As a former CISO, I found that regular, informal interactions with board members significantly improved my ability to align cybersecurity strategies with overarching business objectives. Frequent and candid communication enabled me to present cybersecurity not just as a cost centre, but as a strategic enabler of organisational resilience and innovation.

To foster meaningful engagement and support your CISO effectively, consider implementing the following practices:

- **Frequent Touchpoints**: Beyond quarterly meetings, establish regular check-ins with your CISO. These sessions foster deeper trust and transparency, allowing nuanced discussions about emerging threats, practical mitigation strategies, and resource allocation.
- **Clear Communication**: CISOs must translate technical complexities into clear business language. As Directors, encourage your CISO to frame cybersecurity risks

and outcomes in terms of business impacts—financial stability, reputation management, and operational continuity. From experience, this clarity significantly enhances the board's ability to make informed, strategic decisions.

- **Collaborative Decision-Making**: Engage proactively with your CISO in strategic dialogues, embedding cybersecurity into broader business planning processes. Effective cybersecurity governance thrives on collaboration, ensuring cyber risks are addressed not in isolation, but as integral elements of overall business strategy.

Remember, the effectiveness of your cybersecurity governance hinges on a strong, strategic partnership with your CISO. Prioritising this relationship strengthens organisational resilience and positions you confidently to manage cyber risks proactively.

Cybersecurity Risk Management

Cybersecurity risk management is a critical responsibility for boards. While CISOs and cybersecurity professionals handle the technical aspects, the board's role is to provide clear, strategic oversight. As a graduate of the AICD and with extensive experience as a CISO, I appreciate what Directors require: clear, actionable insights aligned with broader business strategies. Boards must proactively guide their cybersecurity teams, particularly if the CISO may not fully grasp the Director's mindset.

Effective cybersecurity risk management requires:

- **Identifying Cybersecurity Risks**: Continually identify emerging threats such as nation-state attacks, ransomware, insider threats, and human errors. Regularly updated risk assessments are essential to keep the cybersecurity strategy aligned with the evolving threat landscape.
- **Assessing Impact and Likelihood**: Evaluate the potential impacts—financial, operational, and reputational—and the likelihood of identified risks occurring. Collaborate closely with your CISO to fully understand and clearly communicate these risks, ensuring the board comprehends the full strategic implications.
- **Mitigating Risks**: Ensure robust mitigation strategies, including technology investments (e.g. intrusion detection systems, encryption), comprehensive policies, training programs, and clear incident response and recovery plans.

To guide your discussions and enhance oversight, consider regularly asking your CISO these key questions:

- What are our top cybersecurity threats, and how are they evolving?
- How clearly aligned is our cybersecurity strategy with our business objectives?
- What would be the specific financial, operational and reputational impacts of our primary cyber risks?

- What additional resources or support do you need from the board to manage these risks effectively?
- How often do we revisit and update our cybersecurity risk assessments, and what triggers these reviews?
- What processes are in place to rapidly detect, respond to and recover from cyber incidents?
- Are our cybersecurity practices fully compliant with the latest regulations and industry standards?

Implementing these guidelines will ensure robust governance, significantly strengthening your organisation's resilience against cybersecurity risks.

Best Practices and Real-World Examples

As Directors, understanding and applying best practices from real-world scenarios is invaluable. Effective cybersecurity governance can substantially mitigate risks, as exemplified by several organisations that have successfully navigated cybersecurity challenges.

Take, for instance, the ANU[18]. In 2018, ANU experienced a sophisticated cyberattack affecting over 200,000 students, staff and alumni. The attackers, leveraging spear-phishing campaigns, accessed sensitive data dating back 19 years. Despite the severity, ANU's decisive response, investing substantially in advanced cybersecurity infrastructure and comprehensive staff training, turned the incident into a pivotal learning

18 Australian National University

opportunity, significantly strengthening their cybersecurity posture.

Similarly, the Tasmanian Ambulance Service breach in 2021 demonstrated vulnerabilities linked to outdated technology. Attackers intercepted sensitive patient communications, prompting a robust governmental review and a swift upgrade of communications systems. The transparency and responsiveness displayed by Tasmanian authorities underscored the importance of proactive risk identification and remediation.

Drawing insights from these and similar cases, Directors can adopt several key best practices:

- **Regular Risk Reviews**: Consistent and thorough reviews of the cybersecurity landscape help organisations remain proactive against evolving threats.
- **Investing in Cybersecurity Talent**: Attracting and retaining top cybersecurity experts equips your leadership team with vital knowledge and skillsets necessary to safeguard the organisation effectively.
- **Embedding Cybersecurity in Business Strategy**: Successful organisations integrate cybersecurity considerations deeply into their overall business strategy. Boards must ensure cybersecurity risk management is integral to decision-making, investment considerations and strategic planning.

Implementing these best practices positions your organisation to not only withstand cyber threats, but also to emerge stronger, more resilient and better equipped for future challenges.

Final Thoughts: Cybersecurity is a Strategic Imperative

As we close this chapter, it's clear that cybersecurity governance is not just an IT responsibility – it's a fundamental business imperative requiring strategic leadership at the highest levels. Your role as Directors is crucial in shaping and overseeing a cybersecurity strategy that ensures organisational resilience and long-term success.

By embracing a robust cybersecurity governance framework, engaging proactively with your CISO and cybersecurity teams, and consistently prioritising risk management, you position your organisation to confidently face the dynamic threats of today's digital landscape. Drawing from my experience advising boards and serving as a CISO, I encourage you to maintain a Director's mindset – strategic, informed and proactive – in managing cybersecurity.

Remember, good cybersecurity governance is not just about defence; it's about leveraging cybersecurity as a catalyst for organisational strength and agility. Take this moment as an opportunity to lead boldly, to create a culture of resilience and to ensure your organisation thrives securely in the digital age.

The key takeaway for boards is to shift from seeing cybersecurity as a technical challenge to recognising it as a strategic imperative. Only by embracing cybersecurity governance at the highest level can organisations ensure that they are not only protected but also resilient in the face of inevitable cyber threats.

CHAPTER 5

Why Your Organisation Is a Target for Cyber Extortionists

LET ME BE CLEAR – ransomware is no longer merely a technical annoyance that can be delegated solely to the IT department; it has swiftly escalated to become a critical board-level issue demanding urgent attention. Across Australia and globally, organisations of all sizes, from prominent ASX-listed corporations to small and medium-sized enterprises, are finding themselves in the crosshairs of cybercriminals who see ransomware as an increasingly profitable form of digital extortion.

Recent data from the ACSC[19] paints an alarming picture, highlighting a marked increase in ransomware incidents

19 Australian Cyber Security Centre

over the past several years. In 2023 alone, ransomware accounted for approximately 11% of all cybercrime reports, underscoring a substantial shift in Australia's cyber threat landscape. Disturbingly, smaller businesses have emerged as favoured targets, reflecting the attackers' perception of these organisations as lower-hanging fruit, often less prepared and equipped to respond effectively.

As Australia's businesses deepen their reliance on digital operations and data-driven decision-making, their vulnerability to ransomware attacks intensifies significantly. The sophistication of ransomware has evolved, shifting from isolated, opportunistic attacks to highly organised and meticulously executed campaigns. Today's attackers systematically disrupt business continuity, compromise sensitive data and hold entire operational infrastructures hostage. Such attacks not only jeopardise critical business operations but threaten financial stability, regulatory compliance and the reputation of the organisations involved.

As Directors, our fiduciary duty extends to understanding and mitigating such threats proactively. This chapter provides an insightful exploration of Australia's escalating ransomware threat, coupled with a strategic, actionable framework designed explicitly for boards to fortify their organisations. Together, we will unpack practical, proven measures you can employ to govern effectively, ensuring resilience and protection against one of today's most pressing cybersecurity threats.

Understanding Ransomware and Its Growing Threat

Ransomware is malicious software that encrypts an organisation's data or locks out its systems, rendering critical assets inaccessible until a ransom is paid. Cybercriminals typically demand payment in cryptocurrency, complicating tracking efforts by law enforcement and significantly reducing the likelihood of recovering funds.

While ransomware itself is not new, its scale, complexity, and devastating potential have escalated dramatically. The ACSC reported a concerning 15% increase in ransomware-related cybercrime incidents during the 2020–21 financial year, underscoring how quickly the threat landscape is evolving and intensifying each year.

The Evolution of Ransomware

Ransomware attacks have transformed significantly from isolated, rudimentary incidents into sophisticated, orchestrated cybercrimes. Early forms of ransomware were easily detectable and straightforward in execution. Today's attacks, however, often involve prolonged infiltration, with cybercriminals patiently navigating within compromised networks for months, gathering sensitive data and laying strategic groundwork for a targeted and potent attack.

A particularly alarming development is the advent of double extortion. Attackers now not only encrypt data but also exfiltrate sensitive or proprietary information, threatening to release it publicly unless their ransom demands are met. Such a tactic exploits organisations' concerns around data privacy and regulatory compliance, increasing the pressure to pay.

Moreover, the proliferation of RaaS[20] has drastically lowered the barrier of entry, allowing cybercriminals with minimal technical skills to launch sophisticated ransomware attacks using readily available tools and infrastructure provided by experienced cybercriminal networks.

The Financial and Reputational Impact of Ransomware

From a board perspective, ransomware transcends IT concerns – it is fundamentally a strategic business risk. Financial losses can be substantial; ACSC's 2021 data reveals that ransomware incidents typically cost small Australian businesses around AUD $8,899 per incident, medium-sized organisations approximately AUD $33,442, and larger enterprises millions. These figures reflect more than just ransom payments; they encompass operational downtime, restoration expenses, legal fees and potential customer attrition.

Reputational damage is equally significant, often resulting in long-term consequences that far exceed immediate financial impacts. Once compromised, trust (especially when involving sensitive customer data) is challenging to regain. Organisations publicly associated with ransomware attacks risk lasting

20 Ransomware-as-a-Service

reputational harm, which in turn affects customer confidence, loyalty and long-term profitability.

Notable Ransomware Incidents Since 2023

Since 2023, the ransomware threat landscape has evolved rapidly, with notable incidents providing critical insights into the scale and impact of these attacks. UnitedHealth Group's Change Healthcare faced one of the year's largest breaches in February 2024, resulting in a staggering 100 million individuals affected, and a USD $22 million ransom paid to the Alphv/BlackCat gang. Veolia North America experienced operational disruptions, though no ransom was publicly claimed, highlighting vulnerabilities in critical infrastructure.

Other significant incidents include Ascension's prolonged disruption impacting electronic health records and patient care systems, the Port of Seattle's operational outages at Seattle-Tacoma International Airport, and Blue Yonder's attack severely affecting the supply chains of major retailers such as Starbucks and Sainsbury's.

The rapid emergence of the RansomHub group, claiming over 500 victims in just six months, and the Play ransomware attack on Krispy Kreme, disrupting digital sales and delivery systems, further underscores ransomware's pervasive threat and the urgency of proactive board-level intervention.

The Role of the Board in Ransomware Protection

Boards of Directors are ultimately responsible for ensuring that their organisations have appropriate risk management frameworks in place to address the growing cyber threat landscape, including ransomware. Cybersecurity should be viewed as a strategic priority, with boards actively involved in governance and decision-making related to the organisation's cyber posture.

Governance and Oversight

The first step for boards is to recognise that cybersecurity is not merely an IT problem, but a crucial part of organisational risk management. This means incorporating cybersecurity risk into the broader risk management framework and ensuring that there is a clear understanding of the potential business impacts of a ransomware attack. Boards should engage with cybersecurity experts to understand the specific threats their organisation faces. The ACSC's annual report highlights that ransomware attacks now account for a substantial portion of cybercrime incidents, and without a strategic approach to risk management, organisations will continue to be vulnerable. Directors must understand that traditional risk management frameworks may not be sufficient in the face of rapidly evolving cyber threats. Boards should be looking at cybersecurity resilience, the ability to withstand and recover from cyber incidents, as a core part of their risk mitigation strategies.

Engagement with the CISO

Boards must engage regularly with the CISO or equivalent senior cybersecurity leader within the organisation. In many cases, the CISO is responsible for the overall cybersecurity strategy and for implementing the technical measures necessary to defend against threats like ransomware.

The ACSC's 2020–21 report reveals that 35% of ransomware incidents involved inadequate technical defences, highlighting the importance of ensuring that technical measures are in place to prevent successful attacks. Regular, transparent communication between the board and the CISO is essential to ensure that the organisation's cybersecurity posture aligns with its broader business goals.

Effective engagement with the CISO should involve regular updates on the organisation's cybersecurity performance, ongoing vulnerabilities, and the status of incident response plans. It should also involve discussion around the organisation's risk tolerance and appetite for dealing with potential ransomware incidents.

Australian Cybersecurity Act 2024 and Notifiable Ransomware Payments

The introduction of the Australian Cyber Security Act 2024 marks a significant development, directly impacting how organisations must handle ransomware incidents. Under the new Act, any ransomware payments made by organisations become mandatorily notifiable to both law enforcement agencies and the Australian Government. For Directors, this legislative change underscores the critical need for heightened governance and due diligence in cybersecurity preparedness. Boards must now consider additional compliance obligations and ensure transparency in decision-making processes around ransomware incidents. Directors must be aware of the broader implications, such as potential regulatory scrutiny and increased public visibility into their cybersecurity practices. This new requirement further elevates the necessity for boards to engage closely with their cybersecurity leaders to ensure robust preparation, swift incident response capabilities and clear communication strategies in alignment with the Act's mandates.

Mandatory Ransomware Payment Reporting

A critical aspect of the Cyber Security Act 2024, Part 3, is the introduction of mandatory ransomware payment reporting obligations for eligible businesses operating in Australia. Entities exceeding the designated annual turnover threshold, initially set at AU$3 million, are required to report ransomware payments within 72 hours of payment. This mandatory reporting framework aims to empower the Australian Government and law enforcement with comprehensive data to better understand ransomware threats, enabling more targeted industry support and threat disruption. Directors must ensure their organisations are fully aware of these obligations and maintain robust reporting processes. Failing to report within the stipulated 72 hours carries potential civil penalties, though the government initially intends to prioritise education and engagement over punitive measures.

For Directors, this underscores the necessity of robust internal governance practices, ensuring readiness to swiftly respond to ransomware incidents and comply with these mandatory reporting requirements, thereby safeguarding organisational integrity and maintaining stakeholder trust.

Cybersecurity Governance: Board Responsibilities

Characteristic	Governance and Oversight	Engagement with CISO	Cybersecurity Act 2025	Mandatory Reporting
Focus	Risk management integration	Communication and strategy alignment	Compliance and transparency	Swift incident response
Responsibility	Incorporate cybersecurity into risk framework	Regular updates on cybersecurity performance	Heightened governance and due diligence	Awareness of reporting obligations
Impact	Strategic approach to risk management	Ensuring technical measures are in place	Additional compliance obligations	Safeguarding organisational integrity

Best Practices for Mitigating Ransomware Risks

While no singular approach can guarantee absolute immunity from ransomware, boards must advocate for a multi-faceted strategy combining technical, procedural and human-centric measures. Here are critical best practices and questions Directors should consistently address in discussions with their CISO and cybersecurity teams.

Implementing Robust Backup Strategies

Directors should confirm that their organisation maintains frequent, encrypted backups of all critical data, securely stored offline or in isolated cloud environments, to safeguard against encryption during ransomware attacks. Regular testing of data restoration from backups is equally vital. Boards should ask, '*How frequently are we testing our backup recovery capabilities, and are our backups resilient enough to withstand sophisticated attacks?*'

Conducting Regular Security Audits

Continuous vigilance through regular security audits, vulnerability assessments, and penetration testing is crucial to identify and address evolving threats proactively. Directors should ensure comprehensive reviews of software, network infrastructure and user behaviours are routinely conducted. Questions Directors should pose include, '*When was our last cybersecurity audit, and how quickly do we address vulnerabilities identified in these audits? Are we fully patched against known software vulnerabilities?*'

Employee Education and Awareness

Human error remains a predominant vector for ransomware infiltration. Boards must prioritise employee cybersecurity training programs, particularly around recognising and responding to phishing and social engineering attacks. Directors should regularly inquire, '*How effective is our cybersecurity awareness training? Are employees empowered and encouraged to report suspicious activities without hesitation?*'

Implementing MFA[21]

Directors must advocate for the comprehensive deployment of MFA across all critical systems, especially remote access points. MFA significantly reduces the risk of unauthorised access, even if user credentials have been compromised. A pertinent question for Directors is, '*Have we implemented MFA consistently across our critical applications and remote access points, and are there any notable gaps?*'

Developing a CIRP[22]

A robust and clearly defined CIRP is essential to swiftly and effectively manage ransomware incidents. Directors must ensure the CIRP includes explicit roles and responsibilities, clear communication protocols and structured steps for containment, eradication and recovery. Boards should regularly participate in or review outcomes from tabletop exercises. Essential questions Directors should ask include, '*How regularly do we test our CIRP, and are all stakeholders clear on their responsibilities in the event of an attack?*'

Through proactive governance and diligent oversight, Directors can significantly enhance organisational resilience against ransomware threats, thereby safeguarding both operational continuity and stakeholder trust.

---

21 Multi-Factor Authentication

22 Cybersecurity Incident Response Plan

Preparing for the Future: Shifting from Reactive to Proactive

As ransomware attacks become increasingly sophisticated, organisations must move from a purely defensive and reactive posture toward a proactive strategy designed to anticipate and mitigate future threats.

Emphasising Cybersecurity Resilience

The ability to withstand and rapidly recover from cyber incidents is critical. Directors must ensure that their organisations regularly evaluate and strengthen resilience strategies. Boards should actively seek assurances that response and recovery processes are well-documented, thoroughly tested, and continuously updated. Directors should question, '*How robust is our current cybersecurity resilience strategy, and how confident are we in our ability to maintain continuity following an attack?*'

Role of Cyber Insurance

While cyber insurance provides valuable financial protection, it should complement, rather than replace rigorous cybersecurity measures. Directors must ensure that insurance coverage is comprehensive, clearly aligned with organisational risks, and regularly reviewed. Directors should also clearly understand policy limitations and exclusions. A critical reflection for boards is, "*Does our cyber insurance adequately cover potential ransomware incidents, and are we avoiding undue reliance on insurance to address our cybersecurity risks?"*

Through deliberate foresight and strategic governance, Directors can guide their organisations toward greater resilience and preparedness, effectively safeguarding their future against the evolving threat landscape.

Evaluating ransomware mitigation strategies: from reactive to proactive approaches.

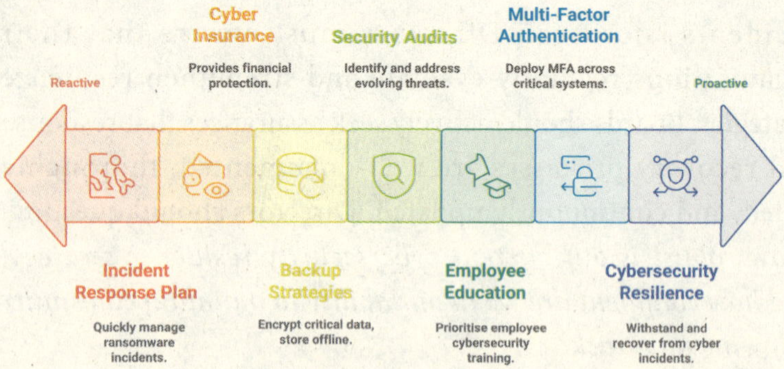

Final Thoughts: A Call to Action for Boards

The threat of ransomware demands immediate and unwavering attention from every Director. In my experience as a CISO, I've witnessed firsthand how swiftly ransomware can dismantle operational integrity and undermine organisational trust. Board members must unequivocally embrace cybersecurity governance as a core responsibility, not an optional consideration.

Take proactive steps now: rigorously engage with your cybersecurity leaders, implement best practices outlined in this chapter, and build resilience into your organisational culture. The time for debate has passed; robust, strategic cybersecurity governance is non-negotiable.

Your organisation's survival and reputation depend on it.

CHAPTER 6

Talk Nerdy to Me: Bridging the Gap Between the Board and CISO

LET'S BE HONEST – MOST Boardrooms aren't fluent in 'cyber'. And most CISOs aren't fluent in Board speak. That's a costly disconnect.

In this chapter, I break down the communication barriers and give you, as a Director, a proven playbook to turn technical noise into strategic insight. This will allow you to lead with clarity, not confusion.

The Pain Points: Why Communication Fails

Cybersecurity has become one of the most pressing governance issues of our time, yet it remains one of the most misunderstood in the boardroom. Despite the headlines, the breaches, and the regulatory wake-up calls, many organisations still treat cyber risk as a technical detail best left to IT. That disconnect between perception and reality is no longer sustainable.

At the centre of the problem is a breakdown in communication. CISOs know the risks – they live and breathe them. But translating those risks into business impact, board priorities and strategic clarity? That's where things often fall apart. On the flip side, many Directors aren't sure what to ask, how to interpret cyber risk, or where their oversight responsibilities begin and end.

That gap is costing businesses financially, reputationally and operationally. This chapter offers a way forward. It's a practical guide to help boards and CISOs speak the same language, one that connects cyber risk to enterprise risk, resilience and long-term value creation. You'll find Australian case studies, red flags to watch for and actionable questions to elevate your cyber conversations from technical noise to strategic insight.

Because when boards engage with cybersecurity the right way, it doesn't just protect the business. It empowers it.

My 4-Part Cyber Playbook for Board Directors

Over the years, I've sat on both sides of the table, as a CISO and as a Board Director. And if there's one thing I've learnt, it's this: cybersecurity governance isn't about mastering the tech – it's about asking the right questions, building the right relationships, and embedding the right thinking at the top.

To help Directors navigate this complex space with clarity and confidence, I've developed a four-part framework, my actionable recipe for lifting cyber capability in the boardroom:

Part 1–The Cost of Miscommunication: Real-world Australian case studies that show what happens when boards misunderstand or overlook cyber risk.

Part 2–The Pathway: Practical steps to build clearer, more strategic conversations with your CISO and shift cybersecurity from technical talk to business dialogue.

Part 3–Strengthening Cyber Governance: How to embed cyber into your governance agenda, align with regulatory expectations and lead with confidence.

Part 4–Crisis Preparedness and Response: Because when (not if) a cyber incident hits, your response must be swift, structured, and well-rehearsed.

These four parts are not theory – they're boardroom-tested, crisis-proven steps to sharpen oversight, drive accountability and ensure your organisation is cyber-resilient at the top.

Each part is unpacked in the sections that follow, with takeaways and real-world insights you can take straight into the boardroom.

Cybersecurity Playbook for the Board Directors

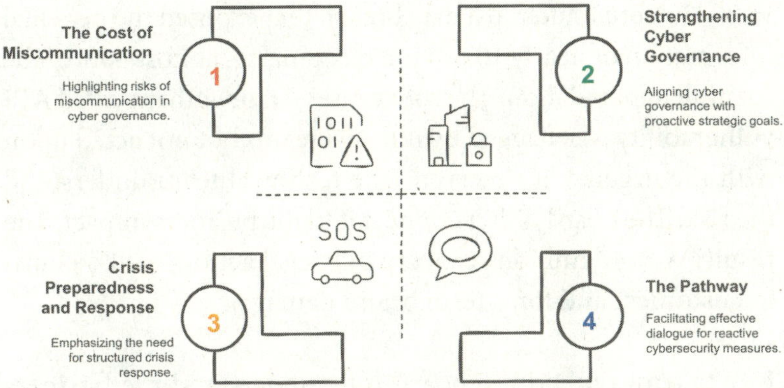

Part 1 – The Cost of Miscommunication: Lessons from Australian Breaches

Australia has had no shortage of cybersecurity wake-up calls, and two in particular should be permanently etched into every Director's risk radar: Optus and Medibank. While the technical details differ, the governance failure is consistent. In both cases, the communication breakdown between cybersecurity leaders and the board created blind spots with massive financial, regulatory and reputational fallout.

These aren't just IT failures. They're case studies in how poor cyber oversight at the board level can damage shareholder value, consumer trust and executive accountability.

Optus: The API[23] That Cost $140 Million

In 2022, Optus suffered a data breach that exposed the personal information of nearly 10 million customers – almost 40% of the Australian population. The root cause? An unauthenticated API vulnerability was flagged by internal teams but not acted upon with the urgency it deserved. The technical team understood the risk. The board didn't connect it to the business impact. The result? A $140 million recovery bill, legal action, a 20% churn in customers and long-term brand damage.

Key takeaway: Did the board fully understand the business implications of API vulnerabilities? Were risks presented in clear business terms, or buried in technical jargon?

Medibank: When Health Records Became Hostage

Just a month later, Medibank faced a ransomware attack that exposed the sensitive health data of 10 million Australians. Hackers infiltrated the network using compromised credentials, an issue the CISO had reportedly raised multiple times. Despite warnings, the board deprioritised action, treating identity and access management as an operational issue. Once inside, attackers exfiltrated personal medical data and published it on the dark web when a ransom wasn't paid. The financial impact was immediate: a 15% drop in share price and a class-action lawsuit. But the reputational hit was arguably worse. Medibank became a case study in what happens when board-level risk governance doesn't extend to cybersecurity.

---

23 Application Programming Interface

Key takeaway: When boards fail to comprehend cybersecurity risks, they gamble with shareholder value, reputation and legal compliance.

MediSecure Ransomware Attack (2024)

In April 2024, MediSecure, an Australian electronic prescriptions provider, fell victim to a ransomware attack that compromised the personal and health information of approximately 12.9 million individuals. The breach involved the encryption of a database server, leading to the exfiltration of around 6.5 terabytes of data. This data included sensitive details such as names, dates of birth, contact information, Medicare numbers and prescription records.

Key takeaway: Was the board adequately informed about the organisation's cybersecurity posture and potential vulnerabilities? Did the board ensure that there were robust incident response and communication plans in place?

Toll Group Ransomware Attacks (2020)

Toll Group, a major Australian logistics company, experienced two significant ransomware attacks in 2020. The first attack in January involved the 'Nefilim' ransomware, leading to the theft and online leakage of corporate data. The second attack in May forced the company to shut down numerous internal and customer-facing systems, causing substantial operational disruptions.

Key takeaway: How did the board oversee the company's cybersecurity risk management strategies before and after the initial attack? Were lessons learned from the first incident effectively implemented to prevent subsequent breaches?

All these cases highlight what happens when boards treat cybersecurity as a compliance matter or a technical distraction. What is needed instead is a risk-based, forward-looking governance mindset, one where CISOs are empowered to speak in strategic terms, and boards are equipped to ask the right questions, challenge assumptions and drive accountability.

Qantas Data Breach Attack (2025)

In mid-2025, Qantas, Australia's national airline carrier, became the latest major organisation to fall victim to a cyber breach. Approximately six million customers had their personal information compromised, including names, home addresses, email addresses and phone numbers.

While a full investigation was still ongoing at the time of writing, early observations point to potential vulnerabilities in third-party systems linked to customer data platforms.

Unlike previous case studies, where delayed, vague or defensive communication worsened the impact, Qantas demonstrated a different approach. Its response was prompt, clear and measured. The airline was upfront about what had occurred, kept stakeholders informed, and showed early signs of accountability in how it engaged with regulators, customers and the public.

This makes Qantas an important counterpoint in this chapter. While Optus, Medibank, MediSecure and Toll highlight what happens when communication fails, Qantas provides a glimpse into what it looks like when the board and executive team get the communication aspect '*reasonably right*' based on the customer and media perception.

From a Director's lens, it's not just a cautionary tale – it's a blueprint worth studying.

Key takeaway: In a breach, silence or spin erodes trust. This was evident in the cases highlighted previously. Nevertheless, in the case of Qantas, a timely, transparent communication was able to limit reputational damage and reinforce confidence in leadership even when the technical root cause is still being investigated at the time of writing this book.

Your Next Move as a Director:

At your next board meeting, ask two critical questions:

- "What critical systems, such as APIs, identity management or cloud platforms, could attackers realistically target, and what would be the worst-case business impact if they did?"
- "Have we reviewed our crisis communication plan in the last 12 months, and does it clearly define the Board's role during a cyber incident?"

The case studies in this chapter reveal a common thread: when boards fail to grasp cyber risk in business terms, or overlook their role in incident response, the fallout can be severe – financially, reputationally and operationally.

Prevention is only half the equation. Precision in communication and preparedness in response must be part of your Director's governance playbook. Because in the public eye, how you lead during a crisis speaks volumes about how you've governed before it.

Part 2 – The Pathway: Building Better Conversations

Recognising the communication gap between boards and CISOs is only step one. The real challenge lies in doing something about it – building smarter, more strategic conversations that move cybersecurity out of the IT silo and into the heart of governance.

Here's the truth: most Directors aren't fluent in cybersecurity, and they shouldn't have to be. But they *do* need to understand how digital risks affect business outcomes, and CISOs need to meet them halfway. The issue is rarely capability – it's translation. Technical risks must be framed through a business lens. And boardroom discussions need to go beyond compliance checklists to focus on what really matters: resilience, risk, and long-term value.

This section gives you practical ways to bridge that divide – how to reframe cybersecurity as a governance priority, ask sharper questions and align cyber conversations with the strategic objectives of the business.

Ask the Right Questions

One of the biggest stumbling blocks for boards? Not knowing what to ask. Too often, cybersecurity discussions default to check-the-box compliance or tech-speak, leaving Directors unclear about how those risks translate into business exposure. But cybersecurity isn't about ticking off frameworks or counting firewalls. It's about the organisation's ability to anticipate, respond to and recover from incidents that could derail strategy, destroy trust or compromise financial performance. That means shifting the conversation from tools to outcomes.

Boards should focus on scenario-based, risk-aware questions that challenge the organisation's readiness and decision-making capability. This changes cybersecurity from a sunk cost to a strategic investment, and it puts Directors back in control of the conversation.

Boards must stop treating cybersecurity as a compliance exercise and start asking the right questions to ensure resilience. In the table that follows, you'll find seven questions to unlock business-ready answers:

Avoid This	Ask This Instead	Why It Works
'Are we compliant with the Essential Eight?'	'If hit by ransomware, which Essential Eight controls would minimise downtime?'	Links compliance to operational resilience.
'What's our cybersecurity budget?'	'What's the ROI of this spend in reduced risk exposure?'	Shifts focus from cost to value.
'Do we have a firewall?'	'How would a breach in our network impact customer trust?'	Connects tech to reputation risk.
'Have we done a penetration test this year?'	'What did we learn from our latest cyber testing, and how are we fixing weaknesses?'	Focuses on learning, adaptation and continuous improvement.
'Do we have cyber insurance?'	'What scenarios does our cyber insurance not cover, and how are we mitigating that gap?'	Encourages understanding of risk transfer limitations and contingency planning.
'Are our vendors secure?'	'Which third-party relationships pose the greatest cyber risk to our operations?'	Shifts the discussion to prioritised, risk-based vendor management.
'Do we have an incident response plan?'	'When was the last time we tested our incident response plan under real-world conditions?'	Promotes readiness through simulation and validation, not just documentation.

Boards must also demand context, not just controls. A question like, *'How would we respond if a critical supplier suffered a breach?'* invites the CISO to translate technical risk into real-world consequences. That's when the conversation starts delivering real value – when it connects back to business continuity, customer trust, and the organisation's ability to bounce back.

Part 3 – Strengthening Cyber Governance

Cybersecurity is no longer just a back-office function; it's a board-level issue that belongs squarely in the governance agenda. In a climate where cyber threats can derail strategy, breach compliance, and shatter stakeholder trust, governance frameworks that ignore cyber risk are no longer fit for purpose.

The challenge? Many boards still view cybersecurity as a siloed IT issue. But if your organisation's future depends on digital infrastructure – and it does – then cyber must be embedded into your broader risk oversight. This means treating cybersecurity as a continuous governance responsibility, not an annual checklist item.

This section offers practical ways to lift your cyber oversight: understanding key regulations, knowing what's expected of Directors and adopting governance practices used by leading boards.

Cyber Governance Begins with Compliance – But Doesn't End There

Let's be clear: cybersecurity compliance is now a non-negotiable pillar of good governance. Whether you're listed, regulated or operating globally, the legal and regulatory bar has been raised. Directors are now expected to understand cyber risks and ensure their organisations are adequately protected.

This isn't about ticking boxes – it's about fulfilling your fiduciary duty.

According to the AICD, Directors must ensure that legal, ethical and regulatory obligations are met, especially when it comes to data protection and cyber resilience. That includes understanding your organisation's risk posture, engaging with CISOs on emerging threats and making sure safeguards are in place and tested.

The message from regulators is unambiguous: passive oversight is no longer acceptable. As high-profile breaches like Optus and Medibank show, non-compliance brings not just financial penalties but reputational damage and potential Director liability.

Key Regulatory Frameworks Governing Cybersecurity

Below are the cornerstone regulations every Australian board member should be familiar with:

APRA CPS 234–Cyber Risk Management for Financial Institutions

Applicable to banks, insurers and super funds, CPS 234 is designed to boost resilience in critical financial institutions. It requires organisations to:

- Maintain a cybersecurity capability appropriate to their size and risk profile.
- Test and assess internal and third-party systems regularly.
- Report material cyber incidents to APRA within 72 hours.
- Conduct annual cyber testing and remediation.

What boards must ensure: that CISOs provide regular updates on compliance and risk exposure. Failure to meet CPS 234 requirements can result in serious regulatory consequences and reputational harm.

Privacy Act 1988 – NDB[24] Scheme

This Australian law governs how personal data is handled, with mandatory breach notifications where individuals are at risk of serious harm. It requires organisations to:

- Protect personal information through reasonable security measures

24 Notifiable Data Breaches

- Notify the OAIC and affected individuals in case of a serious breach
- Maintain breach logs and demonstrate remediation.

What boards must ensure: robust data governance, workforce training and audit-readiness. Directors must be confident that breach response plans exist, are current and have been tested.

Australian Cyber Security Act 2024

The Australian Cyber Security Act 2024 establishes mandatory cyber risk management, rapid incident reporting and board accountability, elevating cybersecurity to a core governance responsibility. It aligns Australia's regulatory posture with global best practices to strengthen national cyber resilience. Key provisions include:

- **Board accountability**: Directors are now explicitly responsible for ensuring their organisation has a fit-for-purpose cybersecurity framework. Failure to exercise due diligence could result in personal liability.
- **Mandatory incident reporting**: Companies must report cyber incidents within 72 hours, aligning with international expectations around transparency and rapid response.
- **Risk management program**: All regulated entities must implement a CRMP[25] that is proportionate to their

25 Cyber Risk Management Program

size and risk profile. The CRMP must be reviewed and approved by the board annually.

- **Supply chain risk**: Directors must ensure oversight extends to third-party vendors, requiring due diligence, ongoing monitoring and contractual obligations around cybersecurity standards.
- **Information sharing**: The Act promotes sector-wide intelligence sharing to strengthen collective cyber resilience. Boards are encouraged to foster collaboration through industry groups and government partnerships.

What Boards must ensure: That it now treats cybersecurity risk with the same seriousness as financial or legal risk. Directors who fail to understand and oversee their organisation's cybersecurity posture may face regulatory scrutiny, reputational harm or legal consequences.

Australian Institute of Company Directors (AICD)'s Perspective

AICD has highlighted the importance of cyber awareness at the board level, recommending that boards include members with cybersecurity expertise or, at the very least, ensure that Directors are educated on cyber risk governance. Despite these recommendations, many boards still lack the necessary cyber expertise to oversee cybersecurity effectively.

Boards that do not have cybersecurity representation or fail to prioritise cybersecurity oversight face significant risks, including:

- **Regulatory non-compliance:** Failure to meet governance requirements under APRA CPS 234, the Privacy Act 1988, and the Australian Cyber Security Act and other regulatory frameworks, leading to legal and financial penalties.
- **Reputational damage:** Data breaches and cyber incidents can erode consumer trust, impacting brand reputation and customer retention.
- **Financial losses:** Ransomware attacks, fraud and system downtime can result in direct financial losses and increased insurance premiums.
- **Operational disruption:** Cyberattacks can halt business operations, affecting supply chains, service delivery and overall productivity.
- **Board-level accountability:** Directors may be held personally liable if they fail to exercise due diligence in managing cybersecurity risks.
- **Loss of competitive advantage:** Organisations that fail to prioritise cybersecurity may fall behind competitors who are more proactive in securing their digital assets.
- **Poor crisis management:** Without cybersecurity expertise on the board, organisations may struggle to respond effectively to cyber incidents, escalating damage and recovery costs.

Recognising these risks, several ASX-listed companies have taken proactive steps to strengthen their cybersecurity governance. Boards should learn from industry leaders who:

- **Appoint board members with cybersecurity expertise.** Having a Director with cybersecurity knowledge ensures that cyber risk is evaluated alongside financial and operational risks, leading to better-informed decision-making.
- **Require CISOs to provide direct, quarterly board-level reports.** Regular communication between the board and the CISO fosters transparency, ensuring that Directors are up to date with evolving cyber risks and mitigation strategies.
- **Implement independent cybersecurity audits.** External audits provide an unbiased assessment of an organisation's cybersecurity maturity and highlight areas that require improvement.

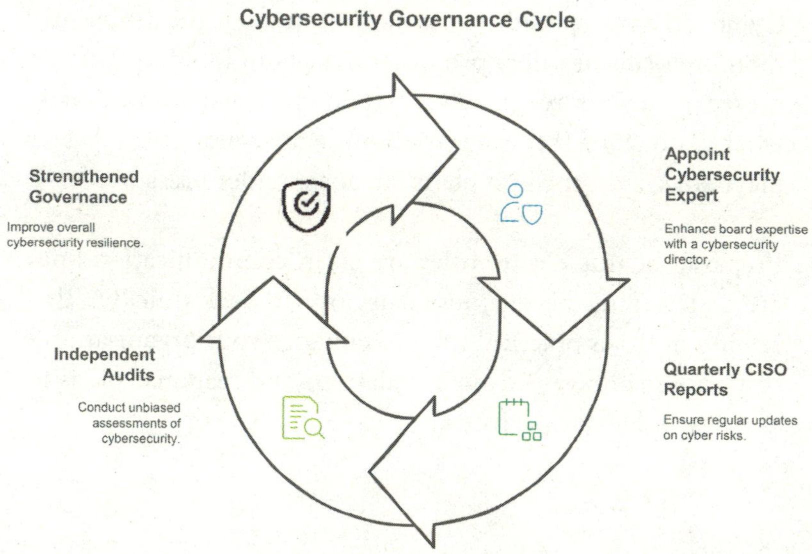

Boards that proactively integrate cybersecurity into their governance structures demonstrate strong leadership, resilience and a commitment to protecting shareholder value. With regulatory expectations increasing and cyber threats evolving, appointing a cyber-aware Director or ensuring board-level cyber education is no longer optional; it is a necessity for modern corporate governance.

Part 4–Cyber Crisis Preparedness and Response

While boards are getting better at understanding cyber risk, many are still underprepared when it comes to crisis response. Prevention often gets the attention, but response planning does not. And when a cyber event hits, that gap shows up fast in the form of confusion, delayed decisions and costly damage.

Cyber crisis preparedness should be treated no differently than fire drills or safety protocols. It's about building 'muscle memory' so your executive team (and the board) know exactly what to do when it counts. Without regular practice and clear playbooks, even the best plans fall apart under pressure.

Prepared boards ensure roles are clear, communication lines are tested, and the business can bounce back quickly. This section outlines practical ways to enhance your organisation's response readiness – from simulations and response plans to metrics and lessons learned.

Cyber Crisis Simulation Exercises

Simulations are one of the most effective, yet often overlooked, tools in cybersecurity readiness. Many organisations invest in defence but forget to rehearse the response. That's a costly mistake. Well-run crisis simulations are like fire drills. They help everyone – executives, board members and frontline teams – understand their roles, test escalation protocols and practise decision-making under pressure. Crucially, they expose gaps before a real incident does.

Benefits of cyber crisis simulations:

- **Faster response:** simulations reduce reaction time when real incidents occur.
- **Sharper decisions:** boards and executives build confidence in high-pressure scenarios.
- **Clear communication:** minimises missteps in internal and external messaging.
- **Regulatory alignment:** supports compliance with APRA CPS 234 and Privacy Act 1988.
- **Team coordination:** validates cross-functional collaboration under stress.

Risks of not simulating:

- **Slow response:** delays worsen impact and recovery timelines.

- **Non-compliance:** gaps may lead to penalties or legal exposure.
- **Brand and financial fallout:** poor handling damages trust and valuation.
- **Leadership gaps:** without rehearsal, even seasoned leaders may falter.

The frequency of crisis simulations should match the organisation's risk appetite. High-risk sectors – finance, healthcare and critical infrastructure – should run them quarterly. Others should consider annual simulations as a baseline and adjust as threats evolve.

Key steps for effective cyber crisis response preparedness:

- Run cyber tabletop exercises in line with your sector's risk profile.
- Test your plans against real-world threats: ransomware, data breaches, supply chain attacks.
- Refine internal and external communication protocols to protect trust.
- Conduct structured post-mortems to apply lessons and continuously improve.

By embedding these exercises into regular governance practice, boards ensure they're not just reacting, but responding with confidence and control.

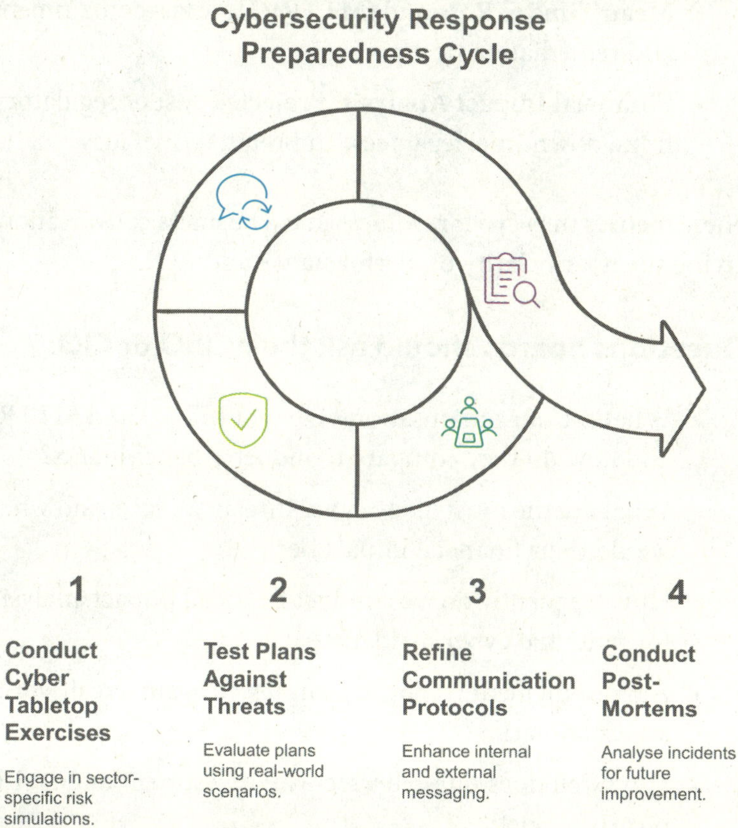

Resilience isn't just about surviving an attack; it's about how fast you detect, contain and recover. And like any other board priority, it needs to be measured.

Key metrics boards should track include:

- **Mean Time to Detect (MTTD):** How quickly incidents are identified.

- **Mean Time to Respond (MTTR):** How fast containment and remediation occur.
- **Financial Impact Analysis:** Projected cost of regulatory fines, downtime, legal fees, and reputational loss.

These metrics turn cyber readiness into a business conversation, giving the board clarity on performance and ROI.

Questions boards should ask their CISO or CIO:

- What are our organisation's current MTTD and MTTR, and how do they compare to industry benchmarks?
- What are the most likely cyber threats we face, and what would their financial impact be?
- How frequently do we conduct financial impact analysis for potential cyber incidents?
- Are our incident response plans tested against real-world attack scenarios?
- How well does our cybersecurity investment align with our risk appetite?

The bottom line is, crisis response is where strategy, governance and execution collide. As Directors, you're not expected to manage the incident, but you *are* expected to ensure the organisation is ready when it comes. Being prepared isn't a technical issue. It's a leadership imperative.

Expected Responses and Linking Back to Risk Appetite

Boards should expect CISOs or CIOs to present data-driven insights that reflect how well the organisation is positioned to detect and respond to cyber threats. MTTD[26] and MTTR[27] figures suggest gaps in monitoring and response that warrant additional investment.

Likewise, if financial impact analysis isn't standard practice, boards should insist it becomes one, to drive more informed, risk-aligned decisions.

By tying these metrics to the organisation's risk appetite, boards can evaluate whether current cyber investments match the company's tolerance for risk. A low-risk appetite demands stronger upfront defences and faster responses. A higher appetite may tolerate more exposure but requires solid recovery capabilities. Tracking the right metrics and linking them to risk appetite helps build a cyber-resilient culture, moving cybersecurity from a reactive issue to a core governance priority.

Emerging Cyber Risks: Artificial Intelligence (AI), Supply Chains, and Quantum Computing

As the digital landscape evolves, new risks are emerging. Directors aren't expected to be technical experts, but they do

26 High Mean Time to Detect

27 Mean Time to Respond

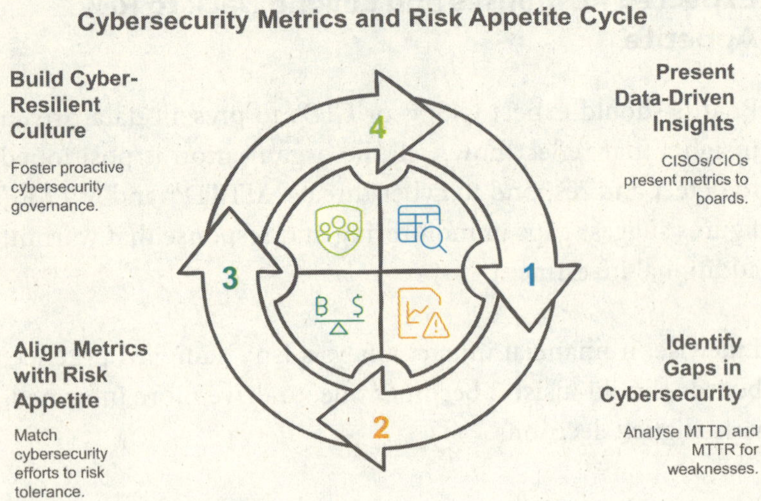

need a working knowledge of these developments to ask the right questions and ensure cybersecurity strategies align with the organisation's risk appetite.

AI and cyber threats: AI is transforming operations, but also arming attackers with smarter, faster tools. From deepfakes to adaptive malware, AI-powered threats are on the rise. As AI adoption grows, so does the need for stronger controls to protect data integrity and decision-making processes.

Why boards should care: AI-based attacks are harder to detect and easier to scale. Boards must ensure AI-driven initiatives don't outpace security safeguards.

Key questions for the CISO/CIO:

- How is AI being used in cyberattacks, and what defences do we have in place?
- Are we implementing AI-driven security tools to detect and respond to threats faster?
- What safeguards exist to prevent AI systems from being manipulated or compromised?

Expected responses: CISOs should outline how AI is being used both offensively and defensively, and where the organisation stands on deploying AI-driven cyber tools.

Supply chain cyber risks: As organisations rely more on vendors and partners, the attack surface expands. A single vulnerable third party can compromise the whole ecosystem, as seen in major supply chain breaches globally.

Why boards should care: Third-party breaches can cause operational downtime, data exposure and regulatory issues. Boards must have oversight of vendor security management.

Key questions for the CISO/CIO:

- How do we assess and manage the cybersecurity risks posed by our third-party vendors?
- What level of visibility do we have into our suppliers' security controls?
- How often do we audit our supply chain partners for compliance with our cybersecurity policies?

Expected responses: Directors should hear how vendors are risk-ranked, how breaches are managed contractually, and whether supplier audits and contingency plans are in place.

Quantum computing and encryption risk: Quantum computing may feel distant, but it presents a very real future threat. Its power could render current encryption methods obsolete, putting sensitive data at long-term risk.

Why boards should care: Organisations need to assess what data would be exposed if encryption is broken and begin preparing for post-quantum security standards.

Key questions for the CISO/CIO:

- What is our strategy for transitioning to quantum-resistant encryption?
- How much of our current data would be vulnerable if quantum decryption capabilities were achieved?
- Are we monitoring developments in quantum computing that may impact cybersecurity?

Expected responses: The CISO should demonstrate awareness of quantum threats and present a roadmap for adopting quantum-resilient encryption in the future.

Linking emerging risks to risk appetite

To govern effectively, boards must view emerging threats through the lens of risk appetite. Cybersecurity is no longer just an IT issue; it's strategic risk management.

AI: Are we balancing innovation with risk? Are AI threats a board priority?

Supply chain: Are vendor risks assessed rigorously enough to match our tolerance levels?

Quantum: Are we planning for long-term data protection, or waiting too long to act?

Key questions for the board:

- Does our current cybersecurity investment reflect our stated risk appetite?
- Are we sufficiently prepared for AI-driven threats, or does our risk tolerance need adjustment?
- How do we balance operational efficiency with rigorous supply chain cybersecurity requirements?
- Are we considering the long-term impact of quantum computing on our data security strategy?

Expected responses: Boards should expect a clear, risk-aligned strategy from the CISO or CIO. If there's a mismatch, say, a low-risk appetite but minimal cyber investment, boards must challenge leadership to close the gap.
By linking emerging risks to appetite and strategy, Directors help ensure cybersecurity becomes a proactive, forward-leaning governance function, not a reactive fire drill.

Final Thoughts: Bridge the Gap

Cybersecurity is no longer a technical whisper in the server room – it's a strategic conversation that belongs at the boardroom table. If Directors don't bridge the gap with their CISOs, they risk flying blind into the next crisis. This chapter gives you the questions, the frameworks, and the mindset to lead from the front. Because in today's threat landscape, cyber literacy isn't a nice-to-have – it's a Director's duty.

CHAPTER 7

Are You Really Secure in the Cloud or Just 'Checking the Box'?

LET'S BEGIN WITH THE TRUTH that is often skirted around the boardroom table: Cloud computing is no longer a futuristic trend. It's here, and it's foundational to how modern organisations operate, scale and compete. From global conglomerates to nimble non-profits, the shift to the cloud has transformed everything from how we store data to how we deliver services. And yet, many boards are still asking: '*Are we secure?*'

It's a reasonable question. But it is not the right one.

The real question is: '*Do we, as a board, understand our cloud risk exposure and are we governing it appropriately?*'

This chapter is a practical conversation with you, the Director, about cloud security, without the buzzwords and tech-speak. My goal is simple: to ensure you can confidently lead your organisation in making sound, risk-aware decisions about its cloud journey.

The Cloud: More Than Just Someone Else's Computer

The term 'cloud' often evokes the image of data floating somewhere in the ether, beyond reach, beyond comprehension. In reality, it's more grounded – and more serious. Cloud computing simply means that your organisation's data, applications and systems are stored and managed on servers located off-site, typically by a third-party provider. It's not science fiction; it's outsourced infrastructure.

A metaphor I often use with boards is the difference between owning a house and renting a well-managed apartment. With on-premises infrastructure, you build the house, pay for it upfront (capital expenditure), maintain it, secure it, and upgrade it over time. With the cloud, you're renting space in a modern, high-rise building managed by professionals (operational expenditure). You don't own the building, but you expect the landlord to keep the lifts working, maintain security at the entrance and take care of any plumbing issues. Your role is to ensure your apartment door is locked and valuables are secured.

This model offers undeniable financial and operational benefits. Moving to the cloud reduces capital outlay, accelerates deployment, enables remote work and makes your organisation more agile. For CFOs and CIOs, it's compelling: no more depreciating hardware assets, no more power-hungry server rooms. But don't let the convenience blind you.

One of the most common misconceptions I encounter in boardrooms is this: 'We've moved to the cloud, so we must be secure.' The truth? You may be more secure in some areas, but you are also exposed to new risks. The board's responsibility isn't to become cloud experts, but to provide oversight. That means understanding whether a comprehensive third-party risk assessment has been done.

- Has the vendor's security posture been reviewed?
- Do they have a tested incident response plan?
- And critically, does that plan align with your organisation's risk appetite?

Cloud breaches do happen. We've seen reputable software-as-a-service providers compromised, exposing sensitive customer and business data. Directors must ensure their organisations aren't assuming risk has been transferred entirely just because the service is hosted externally.

Different industries face different challenges. In asset-heavy sectors like mining or utilities, there's often a preference for on-premises deployments due to capital budgeting structures or sensitivity around proprietary technologies. But broadly speaking, a 'cloud-first' strategy should be the default unless there's a strong case against it. Where regulatory constraints or unique intellectual property are involved, private cloud solutions may be more suitable, offering control without sacrificing flexibility.

Boards should be driving risk-based conversations. The tipping point isn't just about cost or innovation. It's about understanding what you're signing up for.

- What happens if your cloud provider experiences downtime or a cyber incident?
- Do you have business continuity plans in place?
- Have the scenarios been tested?
- Have you validated the mitigation measures if Murphy's Law strikes?

When management presents cloud strategies for approval, Directors should ask if frameworks like NIST or ISO 27001 have guided the assessment. You're not expected to know the acronyms, but you are expected to ensure the right frameworks have been used to inform the decision.

Cloud computing is no longer an IT initiative. It's a strategic enabler, and the board has a key role to play in ensuring that the move to the cloud is secure, sustainable and in service of the organisation's broader mission.

Security in the Cloud is a Shared Responsibility

One of the most misunderstood elements of cloud computing is that security is not solely the responsibility of the provider – it is a shared endeavour. Cloud vendors manage the infrastructure, but your organisation is still responsible for how you use that infrastructure.

This distinction may seem subtle, but it's where many organisations have come unstuck. A striking example of this occurred when a prominent media organisation inadvertently exposed internal documents by misconfiguring a cloud-based storage system. They believed their cloud provider would manage all the security settings.

In reality, while the platform itself was robust, the customer was responsible for setting access controls. Because those controls were not properly set, sensitive files were publicly accessible. The reputational damage was significant, and regulatory concerns followed soon after.

This highlights the essence of the 'shared responsibility model': the cloud provider secures the building, but your organisation decides who gets the keys to your apartment.

As a Director, this is where your oversight becomes essential. Too often, boards assume that once an organisation moves to the cloud, cybersecurity risk is automatically outsourced. It is not. Governance remains in-house.

In another case, a leading university suffered a large-scale breach after attackers gained access to personal data stored in a cloud-based system. Investigation revealed that while technical teams were managing day-to-day operations, the board had little visibility into how cloud security was governed. The result? Blind spots in access control, no regular security reviews and a missed opportunity to prevent the breach.

Security is not a set-and-forget exercise. It requires continuous governance. It requires the board to ask questions like:

- Have we clearly delineated our responsibilities versus the provider's?
- Are we conducting regular third-party audits of our cloud environments?
- Do we receive security metrics that inform us of current risks?
- How prepared is the organisation to respond to a cloud-based breach?

There are practical ways to engage without becoming overly technical. Directors should expect periodic briefings from cybersecurity leaders and ask for regular compliance checks against recognised frameworks like ISO 27001 or NIST. Real-time dashboards with digestible metrics can provide visibility into how management is addressing cyber risks.

Most importantly, adopt a mindset that views cybersecurity not as a technical cost, but as a governance function. Positive framing matters. Cybersecurity is not about fear; it is about trust, resilience and business confidence. A secure cloud strategy can empower innovation, drive efficiencies and protect stakeholder value. In fact, having a cybersecurity expert on the board, someone who understands the strategic implications as well as the technical language, can dramatically improve oversight and decision-making. It's no longer a luxury. It's a necessity.

Cloud computing is not just someone else's computer. It's your responsibility too. And as stewards of governance, we must lead accordingly.

The Illusion of Safety: Are We Just 'Checking the Box'?

Certifications like ISO 27001, SMB1001:2025 or ASAE 3402 can offer boards a sense of comfort – but let's be clear, comfort is not the same as security. These standards are useful starting points, but they are not a finish line. A certificate does not equate to cyber resilience.

One case I'm aware of, involved a financial institution that proudly held ISO certification. Yet a breach exposed serious gaps in their cloud governance, because the certification had become the goal, not the foundation. Security controls were static, risk assessments hadn't evolved with the threat landscape, and there was a lack of incident response testing. The organisation passed the audit, but failed the real-world test.

In another example, a global firm trusted that their ASAE[28] 3402-certified provider would handle everything. When a vendor breach occurred, the board was caught off guard. They hadn't interrogated the depth of the controls, nor ensured regular due diligence on access, segregation or cloud-specific

28 Australian Standard on Assurance Engagements

configurations. The certification didn't protect them from reputational harm or regulatory heat.

Compliance is not security. It signals baseline controls, but it doesn't guarantee effective practice. Directors must understand that certificates are snapshots. They capture a moment in time, not the day-to-day realities of operating in a dynamic threat environment.

So, how can boards move from compliance to confidence?

- **Ask the right questions**: Are our frameworks aligned to NIST, SMB1001:2025 or ISO, and are they living documents? How often do we review them? How often are simulations run?
- **Embed cloud risk in the register**: Cloud-specific risks, such as data sovereignty, shared responsibility gaps, and third-party dependencies, should not be buried under generic IT risk categories. Elevate them.
- **Assign ownership**: Cloud security isn't just an IT issue. Assign strategic ownership and demand cross-functional accountability.
- **Monitor beyond the paper trail**: Look beyond the audit report. Ask for evidence of incident response testing, user access reviews, vendor SLAs and real-time threat dashboards.
- **Frame security as a strategic enabler**: Reframe the conversation. Cybersecurity isn't a compliance burden; it's a driver of digital trust, business continuity and long-term value.

Real security is visible, tested and evolving. As Directors, we must ensure our organisations aren't just compliant – they're prepared. Because resilience isn't built by ticking boxes. It's built by asking better questions, engaging deeper, and never settling for surface-level assurance.

This is not about fear – it's about confidence. And that confidence is earned through governance that sees beyond the illusion of safety.

What Every Director Should Be Asking

Here are my top 10 questions every Director should be asking when cloud security is on the agenda:

Questions to Ask	Insights gained by the Director
What types of data are we storing in the cloud, and how sensitive is it?	Understanding the criticality of the data being stored helps determine appropriate security measures and risk tolerance.
Who is responsible for configuring and securing our cloud environments?	This clarifies roles within the shared responsibility model and avoids dangerous assumptions.
Have we identified which cloud services and platforms are critical to our operations?	Helps ensure that continuity and recovery strategies are tailored to mission-critical services.

Questions to Ask	Insights gained by the Director
What controls are in place to manage access to cloud systems and data?	Role-based access and privileged access management are key areas to probe.
How often are our cloud environments tested for vulnerabilities or misconfigurations?	Look for regular penetration tests, configuration reviews and vulnerability scans.
Do we have a clear incident response plan specifically for cloud-related breaches?	This includes understanding who is responsible, how quickly systems can be restored and how stakeholders will be informed.
How are our third-party cloud providers monitored and assessed?	Inquire about due diligence, contract terms, SLAs and ongoing vendor risk assessments.
Are we aligned with recognised cybersecurity frameworks such as SOC1/SOC2, ISO 27001, NIST, or the Essential Eight?	Certifications are helpful, but what matters is ongoing adherence, not one-off audits.
Is cloud-specific risk explicitly listed in our enterprise risk register, and who owns it?	This ensures accountability and elevates visibility across the organisation.

Questions to Ask	Insights gained by the Director
What reporting or dashboards does the board receive to provide assurance on cloud security performance?	Effective governance relies on timely, understandable reporting, not just technical jargon.

These are not questions meant to interrogate or micromanage the technology team. They are about strategic alignment and assurance. They empower Directors to confidently discharge their duties and demonstrate effective oversight.

A well-informed board doesn't need to know the technical details, but it must know what good looks like. And good governance begins with better questions.

Hybrid Models and Complexity

Very few organisations go fully into the cloud from day one. Most adopt a hybrid model, a blend of public cloud, private cloud and on-premises systems. This hybrid architecture gives businesses the best of both worlds: the scalability and efficiency of the cloud, and the control or customisation that some on-premises solutions still offer. But this flexibility comes with complexity.

Each environment – whether public cloud, private cloud or traditional on-prem – has its own unique set of risks, controls and management practices. Without clear coordination, these environments can become silos of inconsistency, where policies vary, responsibilities blur, and gaps in security posture appear.

For the board, this means asking fundamental questions:

- Do we know where our most critical data resides?
- Are we applying consistent security standards across all environments?
- Is there a governance framework ensuring that our cloud and on-prem systems are managed cohesively, not as disconnected islands?

Hybrid environments also tend to increase the number of third-party vendors involved. Legal, procurement, finance, and IT must collaborate to ensure vendor contracts are clear about responsibilities, service levels and data protection obligations. This isn't just a technology challenge – it's a governance issue.

Boards should be reviewing whether the organisation has a clearly defined cloud strategy that includes a roadmap for managing hybrid complexity.

- Are there periodic reviews of how workloads are distributed?
- Is the cost-to-benefit ratio still aligned with expectations?
- And importantly, does the organisation have visibility and control across this hybrid environment?

Strategic clarity and operational discipline are key. In hybrid environments, board oversight ensures that flexibility doesn't translate into fragility, and that every piece of the digital estate is working towards a secure, aligned and well-governed future.

Vendor Lock-In and Exit Strategy

Another governance blind spot is vendor lock-in. Cloud providers want to keep your business, and some make it technically or financially difficult to move your data or applications elsewhere.

Ask yourself:

- Do we have a documented cloud exit strategy?
- What happens if our provider changes its pricing, terms or performance?
- Can we retrieve our data easily and securely?

The board must ensure that vendor contracts include provisions for data portability, service-level agreements (SLAs) and the right to audit. Without these, your organisation may find itself cornered in a costly or insecure arrangement.

Beyond Cyber: The Strategic Value of Cloud Security

Cloud security is not just a risk management issue; it's also a business enabler. A well-secured cloud platform allows organisations to innovate faster, respond to market changes and scale without fear of compromise. It can also support broader strategic goals like sustainability. Cloud infrastructure, particularly from large providers, is significantly more energy-efficient than on-premises data centres. Some providers are also leading the way in renewable energy use.

For purpose-driven organisations, this alignment between security, efficiency and environmental responsibility is powerful.

When Things Go Wrong: Breach Preparedness

Even with the best controls, incidents can happen. A cloud misconfiguration, a compromised credential or a vulnerable third-party application can open the door to attackers.

This is why breach preparedness is so critical. The board should seek clarity on:

- Who is responsible for managing and escalating incidents?
- How quickly will we be notified of a breach?
- Do we have a tested incident response plan?
- Are our cyber insurance policies adequate and up to date?

These are not questions to wait on until after an incident. Directors must ensure that breach readiness is a standing item in board and committee discussions.

Five Cloud Security Tips for Directors

- **Demand clarity** on what data sits where and who can access it.
- **Ensure alignment** between business strategy and security strategy.
- **Treat compliance as a floor, not a ceiling.** Ask what else is being done beyond certification.
- **Challenge assumptions.** Just because a system is in the cloud doesn't mean it's secure.
- **Invest in people.** Skills and culture are as important as tools and platforms.

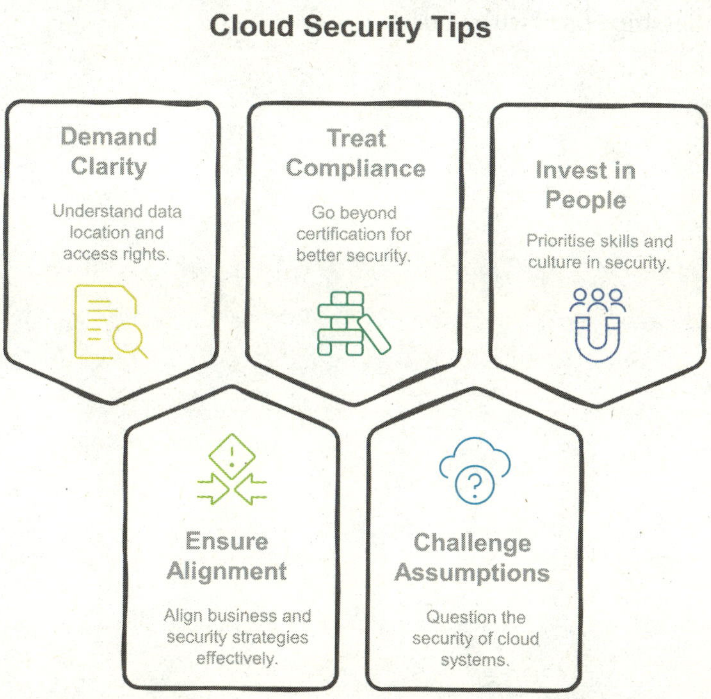

Final Thoughts: Lead with Confidence

As a Director, you are not expected to be the expert on cloud technology. But you are expected to exercise sound judgement, ask the right questions and provide leadership.

Cloud security, when properly understood and governed, can be a competitive advantage. It can empower your organisation to move faster, serve customers better and build trust with stakeholders. But it must not be left to chance, or the IT department alone. Governance, oversight, and strategic alignment are what elevate cloud security from a technical conversation to a boardroom imperative. In a world where data is currency, cloud security is not optional. It is leadership. And leadership starts with you.

CHAPTER 8

What Your Data Protection Breach Will Really Cost You and Your Reputation

ACROSS BOARDROOMS IN AUSTRALIA AND globally, the phrase 'cybersecurity incident' no longer signals a distant possibility – it is a present and persistent threat. For Directors, a cyber breach is no longer just an operational disruption. It is a strategic governance crisis that can redefine your organisation's trajectory in hours, and in the process, expose your personal accountability as a Company Director.

Having served on multiple boards and as an advisor during active cyber incidents, I've witnessed firsthand the disconnect between technical details and board-level understanding. In one board meeting, as a major financial institution dealt with a data breach, the early focus was on system restoration and reputational management.

Only later did questions surface around compliance breaches, customer attrition and the legal implications, by which time, reactive thinking had already cost us critical time.

What concerned me most was that cybersecurity was viewed largely through the lens of IT recovery. The board hadn't yet internalised the broader, strategic impacts – regulatory scrutiny, shareholder unrest, litigation exposure and long-term erosion of stakeholder trust. This gap is not uncommon, and it's why I'm passionate about equipping Directors with the knowledge to lead before, during and after a cyber event.

As Directors, we have a fiduciary obligation to act with care, diligence, and in the best interests of the organisation. Cybersecurity touches every one of those obligations. This chapter is not a technical primer. It's a strategic blueprint to help you understand your legal and financial exposure, the multidimensional cost of a data protection failure, and your governance role in ensuring your organisation is not just prepared, but resilient.

The responsibility doesn't lie with your CISO alone. It starts – and ends – with you.

The Evolving Threat Landscape: Cyber Risk as a Boardroom Issue

In the 2023–2024 financial year, cybercrime reports to Australian authorities surged to one every six minutes. Medium-sized businesses reported average losses of over

$97,000, while large enterprises face consequences that extend far beyond immediate financial loss, including litigation, regulatory enforcement, customer attrition and brand erosion.

These are not isolated risks facing only high-profile, data-heavy sectors like finance or healthcare. Today, every organisation operates as a digital business – from transport logistics to higher education – reliant on cloud infrastructure, remote access, APIs and third-party platforms. This digital dependency brings expanded risk exposure. One compromised endpoint in a supply chain can become the breach that takes down an entire sector.

In this hyperconnected landscape, boards can no longer afford to treat cybersecurity as a delegated IT responsibility. It is a governance issue, central to strategic oversight, fiduciary accountability and the long-term sustainability of the organisation. It is a legal issue, tied to privacy laws, disclosure obligations and regulatory reporting duties. And it is a financial issue, with direct implications for enterprise value, share price stability and investor confidence.

In every board I've worked with, the turning point comes when cybersecurity is reframed as a business risk, not a technical one. That mindset shift is where strong governance begins.

The Legal Responsibilities of Directors in Cyber Risk Governance

As a Director, your legal obligations around cybersecurity derive from multiple sources:

Corporations Act 2001 (Cth):

Section 180 imposes a duty of care and diligence. This includes taking reasonable steps to ensure the organisation has adequate systems to manage foreseeable risks, and cyber risk is not only foreseeable, but also inevitable.

Privacy Act 1988 (Cth):

Under the NDB scheme, boards must ensure systems are in place to detect, assess and notify regulators and affected individuals of data breaches. Non-compliance exposes both the organisation and its Directors to significant penalties.

Security of Critical Infrastructure (SOCI) Act 2018:

For entities deemed to own or operate critical infrastructure, enhanced obligations include reporting, risk management programs and board-approved incident response plans. Ignorance is not a defence.

In ASIC v RI Advice Group Pty Ltd (2022), the Federal Court found that failure to implement adequate cybersecurity risk management measures breached the entity's obligations under its financial services licence. This precedent illustrates that regulators expect Directors to proactively govern cyber risk.

The Fiduciary Duty Link: Cybersecurity as a Core Director's Responsibility

Fiduciary duties are not just a regulatory checkbox; they are foundational to our responsibilities as Directors. They require us to act with care, diligence and in the best interests of the company, and they are deeply intertwined with how we must govern cybersecurity in today's climate.

In my experience advising boards and serving on them, the clearest breakdowns have occurred when Directors failed to view cyber risk as a fiduciary concern. These are not hypothetical liabilities; a single oversight in data governance, failure to question preparedness or delays in breach disclosure can quickly spiral into personal exposure under the Corporations Act.

When seen through a cybersecurity lens, your fiduciary duties demand the following:

Duty of care and diligence:

You must ensure your organisation has a comprehensive understanding of its cyber risk profile. This includes oversight of risk management frameworks, funding of adequate cyber defences and regular reviews of incident response capabilities. Passive reliance on management is not enough – you must probe, challenge and understand the answers.

Duty to act in good faith:

Turning a blind eye to known vulnerabilities or deferring to management without scrutiny, particularly when red flags have been raised by risk or audit committees, can amount to a breach. Good faith today requires cyber curiosity and continuous education.

Duty to prevent insolvent trading:

Major cyber events – ransomware attacks, data extortion and operational shutdowns – can bring solvency risks front and centre. A prolonged outage or regulatory penalty can materially affect financial viability. Boards must monitor and assess cyber resilience as part of their broader going-concern duties.

Cyber governance is not a boardroom luxury or an agenda footnote. It is central to our legal, strategic and moral responsibilities. If you're not actively overseeing cybersecurity, you're not fulfilling your role as a Director.

This is the shift I advocate across every board I work with – moving from compliance to stewardship. Cybersecurity is not just another risk. It's a litmus test of modern governance.

The Real Cost of a Data Breach

Boards often ask: '*What will it cost us if we get breached?*' The short answer is: *far more than you think* – and potentially, your personal liability.

Here's the breakdown:

- **Direct financial costs:** incident response, digital forensics, legal and PR consultants, regulatory fines, ransom payments and compensation to affected individuals.
- **Reputational damage:** erosion of customer trust, media scrutiny, shareholder confidence loss and brand devaluation.
- **Operational disruption:** downtime, supply chain delays, system rebuilds and loss of business continuity.
- **Legal liability:** regulatory investigations, class action lawsuits and Director accountability for failure to discharge fiduciary duties.

In 2024, the average cost of a data breach in Australia rose to $4.03 million – the highest on record. But that figure doesn't account for the true commercial impact: increased insurance premiums, reduced market value and executive turnover.

Directors are not immune. The ASIC v RI Advice Group case in 2022 set a critical precedent. The Federal Court ruled that the Directors failed in their duty by not implementing adequate cybersecurity controls. The judgement highlighted that cyber risk management is not optional – it's a legal obligation.

Similarly, international cases like the Target Corp. breach in the U.S. saw shareholder litigation brought against board members for alleged governance failures.

Cybersecurity negligence is now seen as a breach of Directors' duties. The financial cost of a breach is only part of the story – the personal and professional consequences can be devastating.

Rebuilding reputational capital is harder than rebuilding systems. A single misstep in governance can leave lasting damage. As Directors, we must ask: are we prepared to defend our cybersecurity posture in front of a regulator, shareholder, or court? If the answer is anything but yes, it's time to act.

What the Board Must Do: A Blueprint for Action

Awareness alone is no longer enough. Boards must demonstrate active, informed oversight of cybersecurity, not just in response

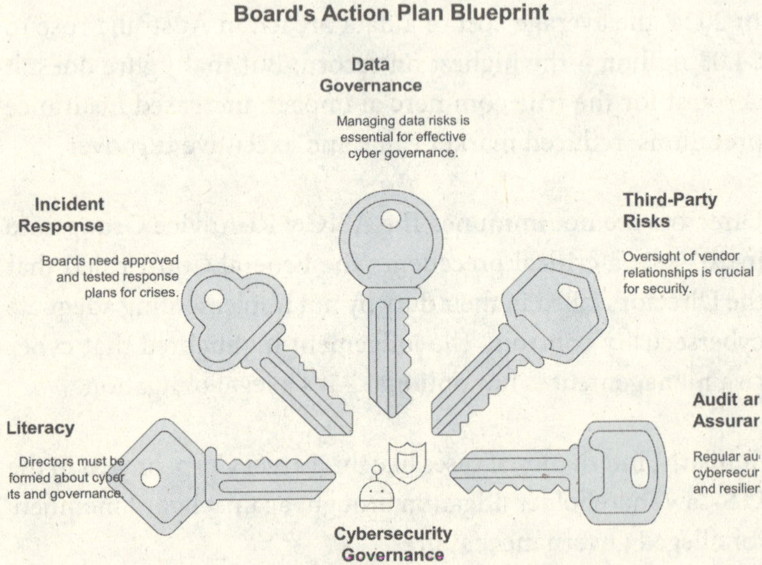

to an incident, but in anticipation of one. Directors have a responsibility to elevate their understanding and governance of cyber risks to match today's heightened expectations from regulators, shareholders and the community.

Cyber Literacy

Cyber literacy has become a baseline competency for all Directors. The AICD recognises this shift, with dedicated training programs such as *Governing Through a Cyber Crisis*, equipping board members with the tools to challenge assumptions, ask the right questions and lead confidently during a breach.

Importantly, Directors should stay informed through multiple channels, including regulatory updates, cybersecurity publications, incident debriefs and mainstream media. A Director who tracks cyber events in the news, or follows regulatory enforcement activity, is more likely to recognise red flags early and question organisational readiness.

Cyber literacy doesn't require deep technical expertise, but it does demand fluency in the most common and emerging cyber threats, the organisation's most sensitive data and critical systems, and the anatomy of an effective incident response plan. Boards should schedule regular cyber briefings led by the CISO, CIO or external cyber advisors, and embed cyber education into their annual board calendar.

Incident Response

Cybersecurity is not tested by policy, but by crisis. Boards must ensure a board-approved incident response plan exists, it has been tested under pressure (through tabletop simulations or full-scale cyber drills), and it covers roles and responsibilities, escalation paths, regulatory reporting timelines, stakeholder communications and mental health support for staff. The AICD's guidance makes it clear: Directors must play an oversight role during a cyber crisis, supporting management, while maintaining independence and accountability.

Data Governance

Cyber risk management starts with data risk management. Boards should understand what data is held, where it resides and who has access. They should also confirm that data classification, encryption, and retention policies are in place, and ensure that data minimisation and de-identification are actively practised. Good cyber governance is impossible without strong data governance.

Third-Party Risks

Third-party relationships continue to be one of the weakest links in organisational defences. Boards must ask which vendors have access to critical systems or personal data, confirm due diligence processes, contract clauses, and liability provisions are in place, and ensure vendors are included in the organisation's cyber resilience planning and incident simulations. Cybersecurity cannot stop at your perimeter. Your risk profile includes everyone you connect with.

Audit and Assurance

Cyber maturity must be independently validated. Directors should insist on periodic third-party cyber reviews that benchmark against standards such as ISO 27001, SMB1001:2025, NIST or Essential Eight, alongside board-level reporting on remediation progress, and transparency in gaps, weaknesses and uplift requirements.

This isn't about auditing for compliance – it's about building confidence in your organisation's resilience.

True governance leadership is proactive, not reactive. The boards that will thrive in this environment are those that recognise cybersecurity as a core business risk and govern it with the same rigour as financial oversight.

The Director's Role During a Cyber Crisis

When a cyber incident strikes, the boardroom transforms from a place of strategic oversight to a nerve centre of crisis leadership. Directors must resist the urge to micromanage and instead provide decisive, well-informed governance. Your role in these moments is not to run the response – it is to ensure it is being run effectively, ethically and in line with your fiduciary responsibilities.

From my experience on boards during active cyber events, the difference between effective and ineffective responses often comes down to preparation, communication and tone at the top. Boards that have rehearsed, built strong relationships with their executive teams, and have understood the broader legal and reputational stakes will be more composed and strategic under pressure.

We saw this clearly in the 2022 Medibank breach. Executives were under relentless pressure as customer health data was leaked publicly, triggering regulatory investigations, class action threats and intense media attention. The board's oversight role in such a crisis is critical: ensuring public messaging remains consistent and compassionate, that obligations under the Privacy Act are fulfilled, and that crisis management efforts do not overburden the same teams leading recovery.

Similarly, the Optus breach highlighted a failure of cohesive leadership. The board appeared unprepared, with inconsistent messaging to customers, delayed regulator engagement, and a heavy focus on blaming technical leads. The fallout eroded customer trust and investor confidence, showing that ineffective board oversight can intensify the crisis rather than contain it.

Here's how Directors can lead when it matters most:

- **Engage frequently with management and advisors**: Stay close to your CEO, CISO, legal counsel and external advisors. Get real-time updates, but don't get in the way.

Ask the right questions and push for clarity on evolving risks and key decisions.

- **Scrutinise communications**: Review external messaging for tone, clarity and alignment. Ensure communications to stakeholders, regulators, and the public are transparent and empathetic.
- **Monitor regulatory and legal disclosures**: Be sure breach notification obligations are being met under the Privacy Act, SOCI and any sector-specific frameworks. Delays or inaccuracies here can amplify liability.
- **Support with independent oversight**: Provide moral and strategic support to management while also maintaining objectivity. Your role is to oversee, not to shield.
- **Track long-term implications**: Crisis decisions must not compromise long-term recovery. Push for business continuity, data restoration and reputational rebuilding plans.

Directors must also recognise the human toll. Fatigue, decision pressure and public criticism can wear down even the most capable leadership teams. Boards must monitor well-being and create psychological safety for executives to operate effectively. During the Medibank breach, the emotional and operational burden on leaders was intense, reinforcing the need for boards to protect people, not just systems.

Equally, boards must guard against scapegoating. In Optus's case, the focus quickly landed on technical staff and the CISO, but the systemic failures pointed to broader governance gaps.

Effective boards ensure that post-incident reviews examine cultural, operational and strategic weaknesses, not just individual performance.

Cyber crises are stress tests for board effectiveness. If the board has rehearsed its role, understands its legal obligations and maintains disciplined oversight, it can steady the organisation through turbulence and reinforce trust.

After the Crisis: Recovery, Remediation and Renewal

Once the initial fire is put out, the real work begins. Boards must understand that a cyber incident doesn't end when systems are restored or headlines fade. In fact, for Directors, the recovery phase is often the true measure of governance maturity.

Effective recovery is not just about restoring IT systems, it's about rebuilding trust with stakeholders, conducting a thorough root cause analysis, managing regulatory response and ensuring lessons are embedded into the organisation's future risk posture.

Let's consider the Medibank breach again. The board's approach during the post-incident phase demonstrated both strength and opportunity for improvement. Medibank publicly acknowledged the breach, communicated consistently with customers and worked to manage regulator expectations. However, delays in fully articulating the scope of affected data raised concerns. The board could have taken a more proactive role in setting the narrative, showing leadership not only in restoring services but in restoring confidence.

The Optus breach offers a different lesson. The aftermath was marked by criticism around communication, customer compensation and perceived defensiveness. The board appeared reactive rather than composed, missing an opportunity to demonstrate leadership in transparency and corporate accountability. As a cybersecurity advisor and Company Director, I believe this reactive posture undermined trust, not because of the breach itself, but because of how the organisation responded in the weeks that followed.

As Directors, here's what the recovery phase demands of you:

- **Commission a post-incident review**: Independent, evidence-based and board-level. Examine what happened, why it happened and how it can be prevented. This isn't about blame, it's about governance learning.
- **Oversee remediation plans**: Ensure they are properly resourced, have clear timelines and are monitored at the board or committee level. Involve legal, risk, technology and operations.
- **Communicate with transparency**: Continue updates to customers, shareholders and regulators. Clarity builds trust, even when the news isn't perfect. Avoid corporate spin.
- **Support the recovery of people**: Post-crisis fatigue is real. Ensure that executive and operational teams are

given the space, resources and support to decompress and regroup.

- **Embed learnings into strategy**: Recovery isn't just about restoration, it's about transformation. The board should actively push for strengthened cyber maturity, uplifted risk frameworks and scenario testing aligned with new threats.

In both Medibank and Optus, we saw how different boardroom decisions influenced the longer-term reputational trajectory. The way an organisation handles the *recovery* tells customers, regulators and investors everything they need to know about its values, leadership and readiness.

Ultimately, recovery is your opportunity to demonstrate that the board not only cares but learns. That it not only oversees, but leads.

Final Thoughts: Embrace the Leadership Opportunity

Cybersecurity is one of the defining governance challenges of the modern boardroom. It tests your organisation's resilience, your board's diligence, and your leadership. It exposes gaps in oversight, clarity in accountability, and strength in culture.

We've seen through real-world examples that the difference between containment and escalation often comes down to how a board shows up during and after a crisis. These incidents have shown us that leadership is not about knowing every technical detail, but about asking the right questions, responding with clarity and demonstrating transparency when it matters most.

You don't need to fear cyber risk. But you do need to respect it. The Directors who lean in, who build their cyber literacy, who test their incident response playbooks, and who support their executive teams with strength and empathy are the ones who preserve stakeholder trust and uphold their fiduciary duties.

Cyber incidents are inevitable. But poor board responses are not. The way your board leads through crisis will become part of your organisation's story – and its reputation.

The responsibility is yours. And so is the opportunity. Lead with diligence. Govern with confidence. Respond with integrity. It tests your organisation's resilience, your board's diligence and your leadership.

You don't need to fear cyber risk. But you do need to respect it. Boards that ask the right questions, demand the right assurances, and respond with clarity and empathy will emerge stronger.

Cyber incidents are inevitable. But a poor board response is not. The responsibility is yours. And so is the opportunity to lead.

Ask yourself: '*Would I be proud to stand in front of shareholders, regulators and the media tomorrow and explain our board's preparedness for a cyber breach today?*' If the answer isn't a clear and confident yes, the time to act is now.

CHAPTER 9

AI is Here, and It's Coming for Your Cybersecurity Strategy

ARTIFICIAL INTELLIGENCE (AI) HAS QUICKLY become the defining technology of our time. It is not just a buzzword; it is a powerful force reshaping how businesses operate, how decisions are made, and how risks are managed.

For Boards of Directors, AI now represents both an extraordinary opportunity and an existential challenge. Across Australian boardrooms, Directors are grappling with the rapid advancement of AI tools – from predictive analytics to generative algorithms – and the realisation that these technologies are already embedded in core business systems. The convergence of AI with cybersecurity, in particular, demands our urgent and focused attention.

As Directors, we are no longer afforded the luxury of being passive observers to these developments. We are fiduciaries of trust, accountability and long-term sustainability. And that means we must be informed, engaged and prepared to govern how AI is used across the enterprise, especially in protecting our most critical digital assets.

Technology is not just accelerating; it is fundamentally transforming the fabric of modern business. Among the most profound shifts we are witnessing is the rise of AI and automation. These technologies are streamlining operations, redefining customer expectations and revolutionising everything from supply chain logistics to service delivery. But nowhere are their implications more urgent or more complex than in the realm of cybersecurity.

In this new era, cyber risk is no longer a siloed issue for IT departments – it is a board-level concern with strategic, reputational and regulatory consequences. The use of AI in cyber defence is growing at pace, but so too is its use in cyber offence. Threat actors are leveraging AI to accelerate attacks, identify vulnerabilities and outpace traditional security measures.

For this reason, boards must take a leadership role. We must understand where AI is being used in our cybersecurity functions, what decisions it is influencing, and how its effectiveness is being measured. We must ask how AI aligns with our corporate values, how it supports compliance with evolving Australian regulations, and how it reflects our ethical obligations to customers, employees and the wider community.

This chapter serves as a strategic guide for Directors navigating the intersection of AI, automation and cybersecurity. It is not a technical manual – it is a boardroom briefing. And at its core, it reinforces the message I have shared in many boardrooms: AI is not coming, it is already here. Our response to it will define our organisations' resilience, trustworthiness and future competitiveness.

The AI Tipping Point

In 1950, Alan Turing asked the now-famous question: 'Can machines think?' At the time, this was a provocative thought experiment. Today, it feels almost quaint. The reality is that machines have evolved far beyond thought. They now learn from data, interpret human language, simulate judgment, and in many cases, outperform human decision-making in speed, scale and consistency.

Generative AI models can compose business emails, generate sophisticated software code and craft convincing digital forgeries with alarming ease. Machine learning algorithms operate tirelessly to detect anomalies in network traffic, automate vulnerability detection and respond to threats at machine speed. In the hands of defenders, AI is a force multiplier. In the hands of adversaries, it is a weaponised accelerant.

We have reached a tipping point. The velocity of AI innovation has eclipsed our traditional governance models. Its adoption is outpacing our capacity to regulate, understand, or, in many cases, even audit its outputs. The implications for cybersecurity are profound, and they are deeply board-relevant.

As Directors, we must recognise that AI is not just a technical or operational topic; it is a strategic imperative. Our organisations are being reshaped by systems that are learning, evolving, and making decisions faster than any board cycle can accommodate. That places a greater onus on us to ensure our organisations are not simply experimenting with AI, but implementing it safely, ethically and with the right risk oversight in place.

Here's the reality: AI systems can be powerful, but they are also opaque. They are capable, yet fallible. They can be precise, but also deeply biased, particularly when trained on incomplete or unrepresentative data. If left unchecked, AI can not only replicate our existing cybersecurity weaknesses but amplify them. This is where the Director's role becomes critical.

Our challenge is to ensure that the same level of scrutiny we apply to financial risk or legal compliance is now applied to AI systems embedded in our digital infrastructure. We must ask the right questions:

- Who is accountable for AI oversight?
- How is bias detected and mitigated?
- Is there a clear escalation process if an AI system fails or behaves unexpectedly?

Boards that understand the tipping point we are at – technologically, ethically and geopolitically – will be the ones best positioned to lead with foresight. The future of cybersecurity will be AI-enabled. Whether that future is secure or vulnerable depends on the governance we establish today.

AI as a Strategic Asset in Cybersecurity

AI is more than a tool; it is a strategic enabler that, when governed correctly, becomes a differentiator for organisational resilience and innovation. In cybersecurity, it holds the power to transform how threats are detected, incidents are contained, and systems are hardened against adversaries.

From an enterprise perspective, AI can:

- Automate threat detection and incident response
- Monitor and analyse vast volumes of data in real-time
- Identify and patch vulnerabilities before they are exploited
- Detect fraud and malicious behaviour across digital ecosystems
- Enhance compliance through automated controls and continuous monitoring
- Strengthen identity and access management systems
- Improve forecasting and prioritisation of cyber risks.

Across Australian sectors, these capabilities are already making an impact. Major banks are leveraging AI to prevent financial fraud in milliseconds. Hospitals are using AI to shield sensitive patient data from evolving ransomware tactics. Universities and research institutions are adopting AI to monitor intellectual property flows and insider threats.

But AI doesn't govern itself. The board's role is not to engineer the algorithms, but to ensure that AI is aligned with the organisation's strategic objectives, risk appetite and ethical commitments. We are stewards of trust, and that trust increasingly hinges on how responsibly we use powerful technologies like AI.

In my boardroom engagements, I often stress that the quality of oversight begins with the quality of questions we ask. Directors must be equipped to challenge management constructively and seek clarity without getting lost in technical detail. The following table is a guide to reframing our boardroom questioning in ways that drive accountability and strategic insight.

Instead of asking this...	Ask this instead...
'Do we use AI in cybersecurity?'	'Which specific cybersecurity functions are AI-enabled today, and how do we measure their effectiveness?'
'Are our AI tools working as expected?'	'What evidence do we have that our AI models are delivering accurate, explainable and bias-free outcomes in cyber defence?'

Instead of asking this...	Ask this instead...
'Who manages our AI systems?'	'Who is accountable for AI governance across its lifecycle, including procurement, training, testing and incident response?'
'Is our data secure?'	'What safeguards are in place to ensure the data feeding our AI systems is protected, compliant and free from bias?'
'Are we keeping up with AI trends?'	'How are we applying Australia's AI Ethics Principles in our cybersecurity practices, and how often are these reviewed by management?'
'What's our cyber risk posture?'	'How is AI helping us forecast, prioritise and respond to our top cyber risks – and how are those insights reported to the board?'
'Are we compliant with the regulation?'	'What frameworks guide our use of AI in cybersecurity, and how are we preparing for emerging Australian regulatory obligations?'

These questions move the conversation from curiosity to accountability. They reflect a mindset shift – from oversight by exception to oversight by design. When AI is treated as a strategic asset, not a black box, it becomes a source of competitive advantage. But like all assets, it must be governed with care, clarity and courage. As Directors, that responsibility sits squarely with us.

A New Governance Imperative

There was a time when cybersecurity was viewed as an operational issue, delegated to the CIO/CISO or the IT department, largely invisible to the board. Those days are over. In today's environment, driven by complex digital interdependencies and amplified by AI, cyber resilience is an enterprise-wide priority and a board-level responsibility.

The evolving Australian regulatory landscape makes this accountability clear. The updated Cyber Security Governance Principles issued by the AICD and the Cyber Security Cooperative Research Centre are not just best practice; they are a blueprint for the future of board engagement. These principles reflect what I have long advocated: cybersecurity and AI governance cannot be sidelined. They must be embedded into the DNA of board deliberations. A passive board is not just a liability – it is a risk vector.

AI-enabled cybersecurity strategies must now be governed with the same level of rigour as financial oversight or safety compliance. This means:

- **Independent oversight:** Cyber risk and AI initiatives should be monitored by appropriately skilled Directors or subcommittees who can bring objectivity and constructive challenge.

- **Ongoing risk assessment:** AI models should be subject to continuous review, not just at implementation, but across their entire lifecycle.
- **Compliance with Australian regulatory frameworks:** Boards must ensure their organisations are aligned with obligations under the Privacy Act, SOCI Act, and emerging AI and data governance guidelines.
- **Ethical review and impact assessment:** AI systems must be assessed against Australia's AI Ethics Principles to ensure they serve people, not just performance metrics.
- **Crisis preparedness and resilience planning:** Boards must confirm that incident response plans include AI-specific contingencies and disclosure readiness.

But governance is not just about policy. It is about posture. As I often remind my fellow Directors, cybersecurity is dynamic. AI systems evolve. Threat actors adapt. And the risk landscape shifts rapidly. That is why the 'set and forget' mindset is so dangerous. AI systems are not static. They drift. Their performance can degrade, their data pipelines can become corrupted, and their decisions can veer into unacceptable territory if not consistently validated.

Model drift is not a hypothetical. It is a board-relevant risk. We must ask:

- How often are our AI models recalibrated?
- What triggers a model review?
- Who validates the outputs and against what standards?

This is the new governance imperative: to move from periodic assurance to continuous vigilance. Boards that embrace this will not only meet their obligations, but they will build resilient, adaptive and trusted organisations in an AI-enabled world.

Embedding Australia's AI Ethics Principles

Too often, discussions about AI governance stop at compliance checklists and technology roadmaps. But as I have found through experience – both on boards and in strategic advisory roles – this is not enough. True governance requires alignment with societal values. It demands leadership with foresight and conviction.

Australia's AI Ethics Principles, developed by the Department of Industry, Science and Resources, offer an aspirational, yet highly practical framework for Directors. These eight principles are not a set of rigid rules; they are a compass for ethical stewardship. When adopted properly, they help boards ensure AI is deployed in ways that reflect public trust, commercial integrity and long-term value creation.

The principles include:

- **Human, societal and environmental well-being:** AI should demonstrably benefit society, organisations and the environment, not just deliver operational efficiencies or profit margins.

- **Human-centred values:** Respect for human rights, dignity and the autonomy of individuals must be baked into how AI systems are designed and used.
- **Fairness:** AI must be inclusive, accessible and free from systemic bias or discrimination.
- **Privacy protection and security:** Data used and generated by AI must be governed by robust privacy protections and cybersecurity measures.
- **Reliability and safety:** AI should work as intended – consistently, safely and with sufficient testing and validation.
- **Transparency and explainability:** People should know when AI is at play and understand its impact on them.
- **Contestability:** When AI makes or influences significant decisions, there must be avenues to challenge those outcomes.
- **Accountability:** Real human beings – not algorithms – must be responsible for the design, deployment and consequences of AI.

These principles are voluntary, but boards would be unwise to treat them as optional. As I often advise, principles like these can act as strategic differentiators, signals to regulators, investors, employees and customers that your organisation operates with integrity and insight.

For Directors, the role here is not to tick boxes – it is to ensure that these principles are:

- Reflected in corporate policy and risk frameworks.
- Embedded into procurement, vendor management and systems development.
- Addressed through employee training and upskilling.
- Actively monitored through board reporting and executive accountability.

Ultimately, the application of these principles is not about slowing innovation – it is about guiding it. Boards must champion AI that is not only powerful but also principled.

When ethical leadership and technological excellence walk hand in hand, the result is an organisation that is not just compliant, but future-ready. That is the standard I encourage every Director to aim for.

AI-Driven Risks: Understanding the Dual Edge

For every great technological advancement, there is an equal and opposite set of risks. Artificial intelligence is no different. In my conversations with Directors and executive teams, I remind them that AI is not inherently good or bad – it is powerful. And like any powerful tool, it can be used to protect or to disrupt.

While many organisations are leveraging AI to strengthen their defences, threat actors are doing the same to sharpen their attacks. The cyber threat landscape has evolved into a high-speed, low-visibility battleground where AI is being weaponised at scale. Boards must understand this dynamic and recognise that AI is not only part of our shield, but it is part of the threat.

Malicious actors are already using AI to:

- Generate highly convincing phishing messages that mimic tone, language and brand in real-time.
- Identify vulnerabilities at scale using automated scanning and AI-driven reconnaissance.
- Evade detection through adaptive malware that modifies itself based on system responses.
- Harvest data from open sources to fuel highly personalised social engineering campaigns.

These are not theoretical risks. They are unfolding across industries every day, at speeds and volumes that traditional defences are ill-equipped to manage.

AI also introduces new classes of internal risk. Its reliance on data opens up significant vulnerabilities. Poor-quality or biased data can lead to flawed decisions. Insecure data pipelines can be exploited, and without proper oversight, AI systems can amplify inequities, embed discriminatory logic, or produce decisions that are neither explainable nor defensible.

In the face of these challenges, the board's duty of care must evolve. We must ensure that AI systems are:

- Secure by design, with data protection, privacy, and resilience built into the architecture.
- Continuously validated, through independent testing, monitoring and recalibration.
- Governed ethically, aligned with both legal obligations and Australia's AI Ethics Principles.

The question is no longer whether AI introduces risk. It's how effectively we govern it.

Boards should actively seek assurance from management on three critical dimensions:

- **Threat parity:** Are we matching the sophistication of AI-enabled threats with equally intelligent defences?

- **Governance maturity:** Do we have the right structures, policies and expertise to oversee AI risk?
- **Risk integration:** Is AI risk embedded in our broader enterprise risk and resilience strategies?

AI is not a silver bullet, but it is a significant force multiplier. Our role as Directors is to ensure it is deployed with foresight, integrity and a clear understanding of its dual edge. Used wisely, AI can lift our cyber resilience to a new level. Used recklessly, it can expose us to new vulnerabilities with unprecedented speed. That's the balance every board must now learn to strike.

Building AI and Cyber Literacy at the Board Level

In an age where data is currency and digital systems underpin every facet of operations, the board's role has never been more complex – or more consequential. If there's one takeaway I urge all Directors to absorb, it is this: effective governance in the AI era starts with understanding. Not the understanding of lines of code, but of principles, applications and implications.

Board-level AI literacy is not about becoming technologists. It's about asking informed questions, interpreting risk signals, and challenging assumptions with confidence. It's about understanding:

- What AI is – and just as importantly, what it isn't.
- Where AI is being deployed in the business, from cybersecurity to customer service.

- How AI intersects with key board concerns, including data privacy, ethical conduct, regulatory exposure and reputational risk.

The best boards I work with are investing in structured learning: convening with AI experts, engaging in scenario-based workshops and ensuring their Directors are upskilled in emerging digital competencies. This isn't window dressing – it's governance maturity in action.

As I often tell my fellow Directors, just as we once elevated our financial literacy in response to global scrutiny, today we must raise our digital and AI fluency. The bar has shifted.

More than ever, boards must demand decision-useful information from management. We don't need algorithmic explanations; we need strategic clarity. We need dashboards that map AI risk to enterprise risk. We need to know how cyber resilience metrics are trending over time. And we need that in plain English.

Frameworks like ISO/IEC 38507 and guidance from Australia's Digital Technology Taskforce provide a solid starting point. But frameworks alone aren't enough. Boards must embed literacy into culture, via committee briefings, board agendas and performance discussions. Because in the world we're governing today, digital ignorance is no longer neutral. It's a risk. And AI illiteracy is fast becoming a governance gap.

For Directors who want to lead – really lead – this is the moment to lean in. Get curious. Stay sharp. And above all, ensure that the knowledge sitting around your board table is as future-fit as the technology shaping your organisation's destiny.

Aligning AI and Cyber Strategy with Corporate Purpose

AI is not a strategy; it is a capability. And like any powerful capability, its value lies not in its novelty, but in its alignment. AI must serve the broader purpose of the organisation – it must be embedded into the mission, values and strategic direction we set as Directors. Anything less is technological theatre.

Boards must take responsibility for ensuring that AI-enabled cybersecurity efforts are not running in parallel to corporate strategy but are fully integrated with it. This means:

- **Supporting long-term resilience:** AI investments should build organisational capacity to anticipate, absorb and recover from disruption.
- **Preserving human judgement:** While automation can enhance efficiency, it must not displace ethical discernment, empathy or the contextual insight of experienced professionals.
- **Embedding into enterprise risk frameworks:** AI-related risks – whether privacy, ethical or operational – should be mapped clearly within the enterprise risk register and actively monitored.
- **Understanding stakeholder impact:** From customer trust to employee wellbeing, the downstream effects of

AI must be considered through the lens of stakeholder capitalism.

Too often, AI is treated as a point solution when it should be governed as a strategic enabler. As Directors, we must ask:

- How does our use of AI reinforce or challenge our brand promise?
- Are we deploying AI in ways that strengthen trust, transparency and social licence – or are we eroding them?
- Do employees, customers and partners have clear and trusted channels to raise concerns, ask questions or flag unintended consequences of AI use?

The alignment between AI and corporate purpose should not be incidental. It should be intentional and auditable. The future will not reward those who simply use AI; it will reward those who do so with clarity of purpose and consistency of values.

As we've seen across the Australian market, resilience is the new differentiator. The most admired companies aren't those that avoid disruption; they are those that recover quickly, learn effectively and adapt continually. That's the mindset we need to cultivate.

AI, when aligned with purpose, becomes more than a cybersecurity tool. It becomes a catalyst for trust, transformation and long-term value creation. That is what we, as Directors, must lead it to become.

Regulatory Landscape: Staying Ahead in Australia

Australia is not standing still. From Parliament House to the boardrooms of ASX-listed companies, the conversation around AI and cybersecurity regulation is rapidly maturing. The release of the Australian Government's 'Safe and Responsible AI' discussion paper and the proposed reforms to the Privacy Act are clear indicators: regulation is coming, and boards need to be ready.

In this environment, compliance is no longer a back-office function; it is a leadership priority. Directors must ensure that governance frameworks are future-focused and aligned to a rapidly evolving regulatory context. This includes:

- Cyber incident reporting obligations under the SOCI[29], which now covers more sectors and mandates rigorous notification timelines.
- Privacy and data protection obligations under the Privacy Act 1988 (Cth), particularly as reforms expand definitions of personal information and strengthen individual rights.
- AI deployment implications across workplace surveillance, algorithmic decision-making and anti-discrimination responsibilities, especially as these intersect with Fair Work, human rights and consumer law.

29 Security of Critical Infrastructure Act

This is not just a legal risk issue – it is a reputational and strategic governance concern. Boards must work closely with management to ensure corporate policies and digital governance frameworks are current, consistent and coherent, and reporting lines are clear, with appropriate escalation paths and cross-functional coordination. Public disclosures must also be accurate, timely and reflective of actual practices, especially around AI usage, cyber incidents and data handling.

Increasingly, stakeholders – from shareholders to regulators and civil society – will judge organisations not just on whether a breach occurred, but how they responded, how transparently they communicated, and how prepared they were to recover and remediate.

The bar is rising. Boards must ensure that cybersecurity and AI governance are not just mentioned in passing, but embedded in:

- Board and committee charters
- Regular agenda cycles
- Risk and audit reporting frameworks
- Capability and education programs for Directors and executives alike.

As I often say in boardrooms, regulatory preparedness is not just about ticking boxes – it is about demonstrating credibility, leadership and trustworthiness in a digital-first world. Those who prepare now will be best positioned to navigate what comes next.

The Human Side of AI and Cybersecurity

Technology may drive capability, but people remain the heart of both resilience and risk. This is something I often remind boards that *the most sophisticated AI platform cannot compensate for a disengaged workforce or a culture that deprioritises digital responsibility.*

Phishing, insider threats and basic cyber hygiene lapses remain the root cause of most breaches – not because technology has failed, but because awareness, training and accountability have not kept pace. And now, as AI becomes embedded in everyday workflows, the stakes are even higher.

AI can be an enabler, supporting cyber awareness through automated training platforms, real-time behavioural risk scoring and predictive analytics. But it can also create new fault lines in organisational culture. Employees may feel displaced, uncertain or uninformed about how AI decisions affect their roles.

Boards must ensure the human dimension is not an afterthought. It must be a core part of our strategic oversight. We should be asking:

- Are our employees trained not just in how to use AI, but in how to use it ethically and responsibly?
- Are we fostering a cyber-aware culture where digital vigilance is everyone's job, not just IT's?
- Are leaders across business units prepared to understand, manage and lead through digital disruption?

We must also assess the broader impact of AI on our people. Will certain functions be augmented or automated? Are we investing in reskilling programs for future capability? Do we have clear, transparent policies on how AI is used in recruitment, performance management and workplace surveillance?

These are not peripheral questions. These are strategic, ethical and cultural imperatives that sit squarely within the board's remit.

Because in the age of AI, trust becomes the currency of organisational strength – and that trust is built person by person, decision by decision.

From Oversight to Foresight

As Directors, we are not merely custodians of today's compliance; we are architects of tomorrow's resilience. The decisions we make in this moment will shape how our organisations operate, compete and thrive in an AI-driven world.

This means we must:

- **Prioritise AI and cybersecurity** as recurring, substantive board agenda items, not annual check-ins.
- **Demand strategic clarity** from management, not just technical briefings.
- **Drive collaboration** across functions, ensuring legal, risk, HR, IT and operations work in concert, not in silos.

- **Support management** in building systems that are not only agile and automated, but also ethical, explainable and trustworthy.

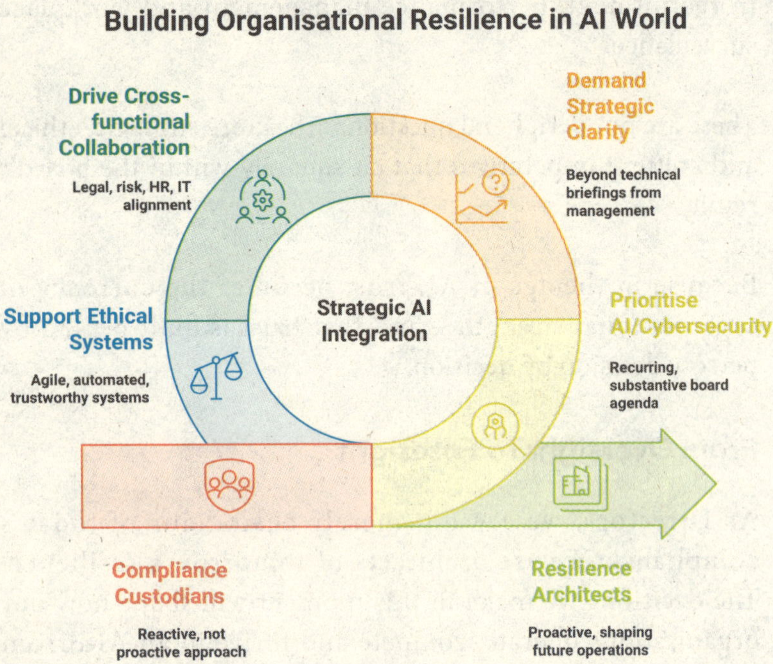

And, perhaps most importantly, we must be brave enough to ask the hard, uncomfortable questions:

- If a breach occurred tomorrow, are we truly ready to respond, contain and recover?

- If an AI system made a critical error, how quickly would we detect it, and how transparently would we communicate it?
- If regulators, shareholders or the public scrutinised our AI governance, would we be proud of what they find?

This is not about being technologists. It is about being accountable stewards of organisational integrity in a time of rapid transformation. Let us move beyond reactive oversight and embrace proactive foresight. Because in the era of AI and cyber risk, leadership is not just about what you know, it's about how far ahead you're willing to look, and how responsibly you act when you get there.

Final Thoughts: Leading in a Time of Disruption

AI is not emerging – it has arrived. It is integrated into the platforms we use, the decisions we make and the risks we face. And in doing so, it has irreversibly reshaped the cybersecurity landscape. For boards, this is not a technology conversation. It is a governance imperative.

Cybersecurity is no longer just an operational issue – it is a board-level responsibility. AI, while transformative, introduces unique risks that must be understood, governed and embedded into enterprise strategy with care and rigour.

As Directors, our mandate has never been clearer. We must:

- Lead the integration of AI into our cybersecurity strategy, not as an experiment, but as a structured, auditable program aligned to our values and risk appetite.
- Demand visibility, transparency, and accountability across AI deployment, from workforce impacts to ethical decision-making frameworks.
- Ensure the board's capability keeps pace by investing in literacy, asking the right questions and fostering cross-functional dialogue with courage and consistency.

The most forward-thinking boards will be those that rise to meet this moment, not with fear, but with informed, deliberate action.

So, let's be clear: AI is already shaping your cybersecurity strategy. The only real question is whether your board is shaping the AI conversation or reacting to it after the fact.

Let's lead with clarity. Govern with confidence. And future-proof our organisations with integrity.

The disruption is already here. Now is the time to act.

References

1. **"5 Ways Boards Can Improve Their Cybersecurity Governance"** – An article discussing proactive steps boards can take to enhance cybersecurity oversight. https://www.csoonline.com/article/3811698/5-ways-boards-can-improve-their-cybersecurity-governance.html
2. **"A Cybersecurity Guide for Board Directors"** – An eBook examining the rising costs of cybercrimes and providing case studies relevant to board members. https://www.thecorporategovernanceinstitute.com/insights/ebooks/the-best-cybersecurity-guide-for-board-directors-and-boards/
3. **"A Leader's Guide to Cybersecurity: Why Boards Need to Lead and How to Do It"** – A resource offering tools, best practices, and strategies to help boards navigate cybersecurity challenges. https://store.hbr.org/product/a-leader-s-guide-to-cybersecurity-why-boards-need-to-lead-and-how-to-do-it/
4. **"Board Governance of Cybersecurity Risk"** – Research on how boards can play a more strategic role in cybersecurity governance and oversight.

https://cltc.berkeley.edu/board-governance-of-cybersecurity-risk/

5. **“Corporate Cyber Governance: Owning Cyber Risk at the Board Level”** – An article emphasising the need for CEOs and boards to actively embrace corporate cyber responsibility.
https://www.cisa.gov/news-events/news/corporate-cyber-governance-owning-cyber-risk-board-level

6. **“Cyber Crossroads: A Global Research Collaborative on Cyber Risk Governance”** – A paper discussing the development of a Cyber Standard of Care through global collaboration. https://arxiv.org/abs/2107.14065

7. **“Cyber Risk Oversight 2023 Handbook”** – A publication by the National Association of Corporate Directors (NACD) providing guidance on board-level cybersecurity oversight.
https://www.nacdonline.org/all-governance/governance-resources/trending-oversight-topics/cybersecurity/

8. **“Cyber Safety Review Board”** – An overview of the U.S. Cyber Safety Review Board, its composition, and reports
https://www.infosecurity-magazine.com/opinions/corporate-governance-cybersecurity

9. **“Cybersecurity and the Board: How Boards Can Improve Their Cybersecurity Governance”** – An article discussing the evolving responsibilities of boards in light of new SEC reporting rules.
https://www.infosecurity-magazine.com/opinions/corporate-governance-cybersecurity/

10. **“Cybersecurity, Audit, and the Board: How Does Board Oversight Impact Cybersecurity Performance?”** – An

article examining the effectiveness of different board governance structures in mitigating cyber risk. https://corpgov.law.harvard.edu/2024/04/16/cybersecurity-audit-and-the-board-how-does-board-oversight-impact-cybersecurity-performance/

11. **"Cybersecurity Books for Board Members"** – A LinkedIn post discussing essential cybersecurity literature for board members. https://www.linkedin.com/posts/mgorge_cybersecurity-books-for-board-members-activity-7021589740722257920-cvls/

12. **"Cybersecurity Governance"** – Resources and best practices provided by the National Association of Corporate Directors (NACD) to enhance corporate cybersecurity governance. https://www.nacdonline.org/allgovernance/governance-resources/trending-oversight-topics/cybersecurity/

13. **"Data Driven Approaches to Cybersecurity Governance for Board Decision-Making: A Systematic Review"** – A paper investigating existing risk measurement instruments and models supporting boards in cybersecurity governance. https://arxiv.org/abs/2311.17578

14. **"Do Boards Understand Their New Role in Cybersecurity?"** – An article exploring the challenges boards face in governing cybersecurity risk. https://www.cio.com/article/3523667/do-boards-understand-their-new-role-in-cybersecurity.html

15. **"Now Corporate Boards Have Responsibility for Cybersecurity, Too"** – An article discussing the SEC ruling

requiring public companies to disclose board members with cybersecurity expertise.
https://news.mit.edu/2024/now-corporate-boards-have-responsibility-cybersecurity-too-0429

16. **"SEC's Hester Peirce Discusses New Approach to Crypto and Cyber Rule Making"** – An article covering SEC Commissioner Hester Peirce's views on changes in cryptocurrency and cybersecurity regulation.
https://www.wsj.com/articles/secs-hester-peirce-discusses-new-approach-to-crypto-and-cyber-rule-making-a6b08432

17. **"The Board's Role in Oversight of Cybersecurity Risks"** – An article highlighting new SEC rules requiring public companies to report material cybersecurity incidents and detail their risk management strategies.
https://www.skadden.com/insights/publications/2024/02/the-informed-board/emerging-expectations

18. **"The Changing Face of Corporate Governance in Cybersecurity"** – An article discussing the evolving responsibilities of boards in light of new SEC reporting rules.
https://www.infosecuritymagazine.com/opinions/corporate-governance-cybersecurity/

19. **"The Cybersecurity Guide to Governance, Risk, and Compliance"** – A book designed to bridge the gap between theory and practice in navigating digital age complexities.
https://www.amazon.com/Cybersecurity-Guide-Governance-Risk-Compliance/dp/1394250193

20. **"The Cybersecurity Guide to Governance, Risk, and Compliance"** – An online resource providing insights into cybersecurity threats and best practices.

https://onlinelibrary.wiley.com

21. **Australian Institute of Company Directors (AICD) Cyber Security Governance Principles** – A comprehensive framework developed by the AICD and the Cyber Security Cooperative Research Centre to guide Directors in enhancing their organisation's cyber resilience. https://www.cisc.gov.au/resources-subsite/Documents/overview-cyber-security-obligations-corporate-leaders.pdf

22. **AICD's Guide for Directors on Governing Through a Cyber Crisis** – This guide offers practical steps for boards to prepare for, respond to, and recover from cyber incidents, emphasising the importance of proactive governance. https://www.allens.com.au/insights-news/insights/2024/03/AICDs-guide-for-directors-on-governing-through-a-cyber-crisis/

23. **Overview of Cyber Security Obligations for Corporate Leaders** – A document outlining the Security of Critical Infrastructure Act, mandatory cyber reporting, and other obligations for critical infrastructure entities in Australia. https://www.cisc.gov.au/resources-subsite/Documents/overview-cyber-security-obligations-corporate-leaders.pdf

24. **Optus and Medibank Data Breach Cases Allege Cyber Security Failures** – An analysis of the 2022 data breaches at Optus and Medibank, highlighting alleged cybersecurity shortcomings and their implications. https://www.techrepublic.com/article/optus-medibank-data-breaches-australia/

25. **MediSecure Reveals 12.9 Million Australians Had Personal Data Stolen in Cyber Attack** – Reporting on the

MediSecure data breach, which affected nearly 13 million Australians, discussing the breach's scope and impact. https://www.abc.net.au/news/2024-07-18/medisecure-data-cyber-hack-12-million/104112736

26. **Latitude Financial Breach Impacts 225,000 Customers** – Coverage of the Latitude Financial data breach, detailing how staff logins were used to attack third-party service providers, affecting thousands of customers. https://www.webberinsurance.com.au/data-breaches-list

27. **Implementing AICD's Cyber Security Governance Principles** – An article exploring practical steps to uphold the AICD's cybersecurity principles, aiming to fortify organisational cyber resilience. https://www.azeusconvene.com/en-au/articles/insights-aicd-cyber-security-governance-principles

28. **Takeaways from the Optus and Medibank Data Breach Class Actions. Insights into the class action lawsuits filed against Optus and Medibank following their respective data breaches, discussing legal and regulatory implications.** https://www.allens.com.au/insights-news/insights/2023/06/Takeaways-from-the-recent-Optus-and-Medibank-data-breach-class-actions/

29. **Cyber Security Governance Principles Refreshed** – An overview of the updated Cyber Security Governance Principles, emphasising the need for boards to consider supply chain risks and data governance. https://ia.acs.org.au/article/2024/cyber-security-governance-principles-refreshed.html

30. **Key Updates to the Cyber Security Governance Principles** – A discussion on the recent updates to the Cyber Security Governance Principles, highlighting emerging issues such as digital supply-chain risks and effective cyber incident response.
https://www.noggin.io/blog/key-updates-to-the-cyber-security-governance-principles

31. **Major Data Breaches Go from Rare to Routine** – An article examining the increasing frequency of major data breaches in Australia, including those involving Optus, Latitude Financial, and Medibank.
https://www.choice.com.au/consumers-and-data/protecting-your-data/data-privacy-and-safety/articles/big-jump-in-major-data-breaches

32. **Total Tools Data Breach Affects 40,000 Australians** – Reporting on the data breach at hardware chain Total Tools, which compromised sensitive information of over 38,000 customers.
https://www.news.com.au/finance/business/hardware-chain-total-tools-suffers-major-data-breach-after-cyber-attack/news-story/0357de37f59744adda85352223ee1830

33. **2022 Optus Data Breach** – A comprehensive overview of the 2022 Optus data breach, detailing the incident, response, and subsequent legal actions.
https://en.wikipedia.org/wiki/2022_Optus_data_breach

34. **Services Australia Data Breaches Surge as Scammers Exploit Stolen Details** – Coverage of the increase in data breaches at Services Australia, attributed to scammers using stolen personal information to access customer accounts.

https://www.theguardian.com/australia-news/2024/sep/29/services-australia-hacks-data-breach-scam

35. **Annual Cyber Threat Report 2023-2024**
https://www.cyber.gov.au/about-us/view-all-content/reports-and-statistics/annual-cyber-threat-report-2023-2024

36. **CISOs in the Boardroom: The State of Cybersecurity for the Top 500 U.S. Public Company Boards of Directors - A Research Report from DHR Global**
https://www.dhrglobal.com/insights/cisos-in-the-boardroom-the-state-of-cybersecurity-for-the-top-500-u-s-public-company-boards-of-directors/

37. **Australia Corporations Act 2001 (Cth)**
https://www.legislation.gov.au/C2004A00818/latest/text

38. **Cost of a Data Breach Report 2023: Insights, Mitigators and Best Practices**
https://thehackernews.com/2023/12/cost-of-data-breach-report-2023.html

39. **Australian Cyber Security Centre. (2023). Annual Cyber Threat Report 2023–2024.**
https://www.cyber.gov.au/about-us/view-all-content/reports-and-statistics/annual-cyber-threat-report-2023-2024

40. **Australian Cyber Security Centre. (2022).** *ASD Cyber Threat Report 2022–2023.*
https://www.cyber.gov.au/about-us/view-all-content/reports-and-statistics/asd-cyber-threat-report-july-2022-june-2023

41. **Australian Cyber Security Centre. (2021). ACSC Annual Cyber Threat Report 2020–2021.** https://www.cyber.gov.au/sites/default/files/2023-03/ACSC%20Annual%20Cyber%20Threat%20Report%20-%20 2020-2021.pdf

42. **Australian Cyber Security Centre. (2023). Understanding Ransomware Threat Actors: LockBit.** https://www.cyber.gov.au/about-us/advisories/understanding-ransomware-threat-actors-lockbit

43. **Cybersecurity obligations arising out of ASIC v RI Advice Group Pty Ltd [2022] FCA 496** https://www.kwm.com/au/en/insights/latest-thinking/cybersecurity-obligations-arising-out-of-asic-v-ri-advice-group.html

44. **Whitepaper: 7 Steps to Developing a Cloud Security Plan** – Navisite https://www.navisite.com/blog/7-steps-to-developing-a-cloud-security-plan/

45. **AI IN CYBERSECURITY - Special Supplement to the NACD-ISA - Director's Handbook on Cyber-Risk Oversight**, NACD https://i.crn.com/sites/default/files/ckfinderimages/userfiles/images/crn/custom/Navisite_Cloud_Security_Whitepaper.pdf

46. **Artificial Intelligence: What Directors Need to Know** - PwC August 2023 https://www.nacdonline.org/all-governance/governance-resources/governance-research/director-handbooks/DH/2025/ai-in-cybersecurity/

47. **Cyber Security Bill 2024 No., 2024 - 2022-2023-2024** The Parliament of the Commonwealth of Australia HOUSE OF REPRESENTATIVES https://www.aph.gov.au/Parliamentary_Business/Bills_Legislation/Bills_Search_Results/Result?bId=r7250&utm_source=chatgpt.com

48. **FACTSHEET - Mandatory ransomware payment reporting** – Australian Government https://www.homeaffairs.gov.au/cyber-security-subsite/files/factsheet-ransomware-payment-reporting.pdf?utm_source=chatgpt.com

49. **Overview of Cyber Security Obligations for Corporate Leaders Leadership in Cyber Security Governance** – Australian Government Department of Home Affairs https://www.cisc.gov.au/resources-subsite/Documents/overview-cyber-security-obligations-corporate-leaders.pdf?utm_source=chatgpt.com

50. **Impact Lab 2021 report** https://www.impactlab.com/2021/02/24/cybercrime-to-cost-over-10-trillion-annually-by-2025/

About the Author

Dr Kiran Kewalramani, better known in the industry as "Dr KK", is a leading voice in cybersecurity and technology strategy, known for demystifying complex cyber risks and translating them into plain, actionable insights for boards, executives, and business leaders.

As the Founder and CEO of *Cyber Ethos*, a nationally recognised cybersecurity advisory firm, Dr KK brings over two decades of experience advising government, enterprise, and high-growth organisations across Australia and the Asia-Pacific region.

A trusted boardroom advisor and former CIO/CISO, Dr KK has been recognised as one of Australia's Top 50 CIOs and was recently awarded *Cybersecurity Entrepreneur of the Year 2025* at the prestigious *Fluxx Awards* in Hong Kong. His perspectives are regularly featured on the *ABC Radio Breakfast* show, and his thought leadership has been published across respected outlets, including the *Australian Business Journal, Business Review Australia, Auspreneur,* and *The Big Smoke.*

Dr KK is a compelling and grounded speaker who has delivered impactful keynotes and facilitated strategic sessions with:

- Company directors and audit & risk committees.
- Executive leadership teams and transformation programs.
- Government and regulatory forums.
- Industry conferences and virtual webinars.

His speaking topics span:

- Boardroom cybersecurity governance and director accountability.
- Navigating the Australian Cybersecurity Act and SOCI Act.
- AI and data security: risks, realities and regulatory pressure.
- Cyber crisis response and reputational risk mitigation.
- Building a cyber-aware culture in every corner of the organisation.

Whether addressing a boardroom or a national/international conference stage, Dr KK speaks with clarity, urgency, and credibility, arming audiences with the insights they need to lead with confidence in an era of digital disruption.

Speaking Enquiries:
Kiran@cyberethos.com.au
www.kirankewalramani.com | www.cyberethos.com.au
LinkedIn – Dr Kiran Kewalramani | Linkedin – Cyber Ethos
YouTube | Cyber Ethos

Offers

4 OFFERS FOR BOARD-LEVEL IMPACT

1. Appoint Dr Kiran Kewalramani to your board or committee.

If your board needs a Director who brings immediate strength in cybersecurity governance, AI oversight and digital risk strategy, look no further. Dr Kiran Kewalramani is available for Board Director, advisory board, or audit and risk committee roles. He brings unmatched experience translating complex cyber risks into clear, actionable board decisions. Protect your organisation and your legacy with trusted cyber leadership at the table.

2. Engage Dr Kiran as the Speaker at Your Next Board Meeting or Risk Workshop

Want to cut through the noise and bring clarity to the Boardroom? Dr Kiran delivers high-impact, plain-English briefings on cybersecurity risk, AI governance, and technology trends tailored for Directors and Executives. Whether it's a half a day engagement or a deep-dive strategic workshop, Dr Kiran helps Boards see what matters and what to do next. Trusted by Chairs, Audit Committees and CEOs alike, his sessions are insightful, actionable, and never generic. Equip your Board with the language, confidence, and focus to lead in a volatile digital landscape.

3. Engage Dr Kiran as your fractional CISO or CIO.

Not ready for a full-time executive? Dr Kiran can step in as your fractional Chief Information Security Officer (CISO) or CIO, offering the board and executive team exactly what they need: visibility, confidence and control. From board reporting to incident readiness, Dr Kiran will help you close the gap between cybersecurity uncertainty and strategic clarity. Get expert guidance without the overhead – just smart, sharp, tailored leadership.

4. Partner with Cyber Ethos for cybersecurity services.

Cyber Ethos is the award-winning cybersecurity firm founded by Dr Kiran Kewalramani. From boardroom education and cyber maturity assessments to policy design, risk audits, and incident response planning, Cyber Ethos is your trusted partner in lifting organisational cyber resilience. Whether you're an ASX-listed entity or a not-for-profit, we help boards sleep better at night. Explore our services at www.cyberethos.com.au

BONUS: Request a free board cybersecurity audit.

Not sure where your Board stands on cyber readiness? Dr Kiran is offering a complimentary board cybersecurity audit to assess your governance posture, exposure and incident preparedness. It's fast, high-impact, and risk-free, and just might be the wake-up call your board needs. To book your free audit, contact Dr Kiran directly: kirank.ned@gmail.com or at www.linkedin.com/in/kirankewalramani

Media Bio

Dr Kiran Kewalramani is the CEO and Founder of *Cyber Ethos*, a cybersecurity firm known for cutting through the jargon to deliver smart, risk-based protection for Australian organisations. With over two decades of experience, Kiran has led digital security overhauls for government, education, and SMEs, making him a go-to expert for media and industry alike.

Named one of Australia's Top 50 CIOs, and winner of the 2025 *Cybersecurity Entrepreneur of the Year*, he's been featured on *ABC Radio* and in national business publications. Kiran is also a mentor and advocate for emerging talent in the field, helping shape the next wave of cybersecurity leadership.